The History of Accounting

The History of Accounting

AUDITORS

THEIR DUTIES AND RESPONSIBILITIES

Francis W[illiam] Pixley

ARNO PRESS

A New York Times Company

New York — 1976

Editorial Supervision: SHEILA MEHLMAN

———◆———

Reprint Edition 1976 by Arno Press Inc.

Reprinted from a copy in the Harvard University
Law School Library

THE HISTORY OF ACCOUNTING
ISBN for complete set: 0-405-07540-5
See last pages of this volume for titles.

Manufactured in the United States of America

———◆———

Library of Congress Cataloging in Publication Data

Pixley, Francis William, 1852-1933.
    Auditors, their duties and responsibilities.

    (The History of accounting)
    Reprint of the 1881 ed. published by E. Wilson,
London.
    1. Auditors--Legal status, laws, etc.--Great Britain.
I. Title. II. Series.
KD2974.P58   344'.41'0176165745   75-18480
ISBN 0-405-07562-6

AUDITORS.

AUDITORS:

THEIR DUTIES AND RESPONSIBILITIES

UNDER THE

JOINT-STOCK COMPANIES ACTS

AND THE

FRIENDLY SOCIETIES AND INDUSTRIAL AND PROVIDENT SOCIETIES ACTS.

BY

FRANCIS W. PIXLEY

(Of the Firm of Chandler, Pixley, and Co.),

A FELLOW OF THE INSTITUTE OF CHARTERED ACCOUNTANTS IN ENGLAND
AND WALES.

LONDON:

EFFINGHAM WILSON, ROYAL EXCHANGE.

1881.

PRINTED BY EFFINGHAM WILSON, ROYAL EXCHANGE.

PREFACE.

ALTHOUGH for many years it has been the custom for the Accounts of Joint-Stock Companies to be examined and certified by Auditors before they are presented to the Shareholders for their approval and adoption, there has not hitherto appeared any work embracing the principles, practice, and general information relative to their duties.

This Treatise has therefore been written with the hope that it will supply a want to those who periodically audit the Accounts of Public Companies registered under the vàrious Acts of Parliament.

As almost every description of business is transacted by these Companies, it would be impossible to discuss all the items which appear in their published Accounts. In the following pages, therefore, a selection has been made of those which most frequently come under the observation of Auditors, the remarks relative to which will be of assistance in those instances when the items respecting which an Auditor requires information have not been separately treated.

The method of performing an audit cannot be arbitrarily prescribed by rules to be followed by Auditors as a class. It must necessarily vary according to the experience of the Auditor and the nature of the business of the Company whose Accounts it is his duty to investigate. In all cases, however, the audit should be conducted on a system, and the author has therefore considered it necessary to enter into certain details with the object of guiding an Auditor throughout the prosecution of his audit. The remarks, however, must be looked upon as merely suggestions which experience has shown are practicable, and it must be understood the author has not any intention of appearing to instruct professional Auditors as to the manner in which their duties should be performed.

He trusts, however, this work will be acceptable to members of his own profession, and that it will be useful as a book of reference to them, as well as to others who fill the important appointments of Auditors of Joint-Stock Companies.

LONDON;
27th January, 1881.

CONTENTS.

CHAPTER I.

INTRODUCTORY.

CHAPTER II.

MODE OF APPOINTMENT OF AUDITORS.

CHAPTER III.

CHAPTER IV.

CHAPTER V.

NATURE AND PRINCIPLES OF AN AUDIT.

CHAPTER VI.

FORMS OF ACCOUNTS PUBLISHED BY COMPANIES.

CHAPTER VII.

THE REVENUE ACCOUNT.

CHAPTER VIII.

THE BALANCE SHEET.

CHAPTER IX.

FURTHER REMARKS ON THE DUTIES AND RESPONSIBILITIES OF AUDITORS.

APPENDIX A.

CONTENTS.

APPENDIX B.

INDEX OF SECTIONS OF THE STATUTES.

AUDITORS:

DUTIES AND RESPONSIBILITIES.

CHAPTER I.

INTRODUCTORY.

History of Statutory Law relating to Joint-Stock Companies—
General Management of Companies in hands of the Directors—Periodical Meetings of the Shareholders—Statement
of Accounts laid before these Meetings—Accounts previously audited by Representative of the Shareholders.

Since the 2nd day of November, 1862, the day on which the Companies Act, 1862, came into operation, there has been a marked increase in the number of Associations formed for enabling persons of all classes, trades, and denominations to combine together for the purpose of carrying on to their mutual advantage a single trade or any enterprise for the development of which the joint-stock principle, as amended by the new Act, offered improved facilities.

Increase of Joint Stock Companies since 2nd November, 1862.

For a considerable time previous to the passing of this Act these Associations had been in existence, but until 1844 they were subject to the law which governed ordinary partnerships of two or three

1

persons, and the Promoters of Railway and other Companies had the entire charge of their undertakings, made contracts with Landowners and others, and issued prospectuses, on the faith of which subscriptions were received and certificates of shares issued without interference or control on the part of the Legislature.

Joint Stock Companies Registration Act, 1844.

The first Joint Stock Companies Act (called the Joint Stock Companies Registration Act) was passed in 1844, and it remained in force until 1856, when it was repealed, except as respected Insurance Companies, for which Companies it remained in force until the Companies Act, 1862, came into operation.

The first Act of Parliament making limited liability attainable by Joint Stock Companies was passed in 1855, but this was not brought forward as an independent measure, and was, in fact, merely a graft on the Act of 1844.

Joint Stock Companies Act, 1856.

In 1856, however, Mr. Robert Lowe, who was at that time the Vice-President of the Board of Trade, brought into the House of Commons the Joint Stock Companies Act, 1856, which repealed the previous Acts referred to, and reduced their provisions into a practical system. In 1857 and 1858 four additional Acts were passed, and in order to consolidate the Acts relating to Joint Stock Companies Lord Chelmsford brought a fresh one in twice in 1859, but it did not pass, neither was Lord Campbell more successful in 1860. In 1862, however, the Act now in force (25 and 26 Vic., c. 89) was passed which has given so great an impetus to Joint Stock enterprise.

Companies Act, 1862.

In addition to the Companies registered under the Act of 1862, there are those registered under various other public Acts, as also those incorporated by special Acts of Parliament. The latter are, of course, subject to certain public Acts in addition to their own private ones.

The majority of Companies are, however, registered under the Act of 1862; and these Associations, known generally under the name of Limited Companies (although the Act of 1862 provides for the incorporation and management of unlimited Companies), have invaded almost every department of commerce and trade, and the capital embarked in these undertakings is enormous.

Every class of persons who have either inherited or acquired means, even down to the artisan, who out of his wages has saved a few pounds, is interested in the management and welfare of one or more of these Associations, and every person holding a share is consequently a partner in each one in which he is a Shareholder.

As, however, it would be impossible for each of the partners in these undertakings to have a voice in the general management of the business, in the same manner as have the partners in a private firm, it is the practice to delegate this power to a few (varying according to the size and the nature of the business of the Company) of their number, now generally styled Directors, who undertake the superintendence and the administration of the affairs of the Company on behalf of themselves, and of their co-partners.

Meetings of Shareholders.

The Directors have periodically to meet the general body of Shareholders, for the purpose of accounting to them the manner in which they have fulfilled their duties. If these have been performed to the satisfaction of the Shareholders, they usually continue the Directors in their position, but should the former be dissatisfied with their representatives, they elect others out of their body to take the place of the Directors who retire by rotation, it being the custom for about a third or a quarter of the Board to vacate their seats annually, in order to give the Shareholders the opportunity of introducing fresh representatives should they consider a change in the administration desirable.

Usually held yearly or half-yearly, at which accounts are submitted.

The meetings of the Shareholders are almost invariably held yearly or half yearly, and it is now the recognised practice for accounts to be prepared showing the result of the transactions of the Company since the previous meeting (or, if the Company be a new one, since its incorporation), and for these accounts to be printed and sent to all the Shareholders, in conjunction with a Report of the Directors and a notice convening the meeting.

The Shareholders have therefore the opportunity of ascertaining what have been the transactions of their undertaking since its incorporation, or their last meeting, and of considering, before they are brought together, what steps, if any, they shall take at the meeting, supposing the facts as disclosed by the accounts, and the report of the Directors, are not satisfactory.

As it would be impossible in many instances, and very inconvenient in all, for each partner to examine these Statements of Accounts with the Books kept at the offices of the Company, and, frequently elsewhere, their correctness is usually certified by their representative or representatives, elected annually, for the purpose of ascertaining that the funds of the Company have been properly accounted for, that such of them as have been expended have been applied in the manner indicated in the accounts, that the unexpended portion is invested as stated in the Accounts, and generally that, in their opinion, the Accounts, as put forward by the Directors for adoption by their co-partners, are accurate in every respect, and to be relied on as showing the result of their management and the true position of their Company, as set forth in the statement of its liabilities and assets.

This representative of the Shareholders is known as the Auditor of the Company, and the object of this treatise is to point out the duties and responsibilities of those who have to investigate the Books and Affairs of a Company, before the accounts, as prepared by the Directors, are placed before the Shareholders at their periodical meetings for their approval, confirmation, and adoption.

It is evident that the duties of an Auditor are not only onerous and responsible, but frequently intricate, and at times even disagreeable. It may happen that he differs with the Directors as to the manner in which the Accounts should be stated, or as to other matters connected with his office. As the representative of the Shareholders, his principal obligation is, of course, to have regard to their interests, and though he may be accused, by the Directors, of interfering with what they may consider their own particular duties, he should not allow their arguments to persuade him when he feels sure his suggested alterations would, if carried out, be beneficial to the general body of the Shareholders.

Usually on good terms with them. As a rule, however, Directors are men of honour and integrity, and when that is the case, an Auditor will find his occupation easy and pleasant to perform. He will obtain ready access to all Books, Documents, and Securities, and every facility will be afforded him in the prosecution of his audit. Any queries he may raise will be immediately and satisfactorily answered, and any suggestions he may make for an alteration in the mode of keeping the Books or in the Accounts submitted to him for confirmation, will be carefully considered, and if approved of as likely to prove advantageous on adoption will be ordered to be carried out.

Except when they have neglected their duty. If, on the other hand, the Directors have neglected their duties or have intentionally prepared false Accounts to be laid before the Shareholders, the Auditor has a very unpleasant and often difficult task before him. Every possible obstacle is thrown in his way to prevent his discovering and exposing their intended deceptions, but the Auditor should be firm, should require all his questions answered, and each unsatisfactory item explained before he affixes his Certificate to the Accounts. He should not allow himself to be tired out and hurried into signing them before he is thoroughly satisfied they are absolutely and entirely correct. The Directors are in his power if he be firm, as they would be placed in an embarrassing position if they attempted to face the meeting of the Shareholders without the Auditor's Certificate.

The Shareholders of a Company may therefore be said to have two representatives of their interests, the one administrative, as represented by the Directors, the other critical, in the person of their Auditor. The latter is therefore a kind of check on the former, and frequently prevents the Directors from acting impulsively or recklessly, they knowing their transactions will ultimately be reviewed calmly and impartially by the Auditor, who will communicate the result of his investigation and criticism to the Shareholders, to be acted upon by them as they may think proper at their Meeting.

Shareholders have two representatives.

It is apparent, therefore, as before stated, that the Auditor has it in his power to render great and important services to the Shareholders, and the object of the author is to provide those appointed to this office with a handbook for reference on those points which most frequently require their attention and examination.

As to how far the Auditors are the Agents of the Shareholders, Mr. H. Burton Buckley, in his work on the 'Companies Acts' (3rd edition, p. 420), makes the following remarks:

" The Auditors are Agents of the Shareholders so far as relates to the Audit of the Accounts, and

Auditors, how far Shareholders' Agents.

for the purpose of the Audit they will bind the Shareholders. But they are not the Agents of the Shareholders, so as to conclude the Shareholders by any knowledge which in the course of the Audit they may have acquired of any unauthorised acts on the part of the Directors. It is no part of their office to inquire into the validity of any transaction appearing in the Accounts of the Company (Spackman *v.* Evans, L. R. 3, H. L. 171, 196, 236).

Opinion of Lord Justice Turner.

"It was said by Lord Justice Turner, in Nicol's case (3 De G., and J. 387, 441), with respect to fraudulent representations made by the Directors as to the position of the Company, that 'there were Auditors of the Company appointed by the Shareholders. These Auditors were within the scope of their duty, at least as much the Agents of the Shareholders as the Directors were, and the false and fraudulent representations were discoverable by them.' But

Opinion of Lord Chelmsford.

Lord Chelmsford, in Spackman *v.* Evans (L. R. 3, H. L. 171, 236), expressed himself as unable to concur with the Lord Justice in treating the Auditors as the Agents of the Shareholders for that purpose."

CHAPTER II.

MODE OF APPOINTMENT OF AUDITORS.

Audit of Accounts of Companies registered under Companies Act, 1862, not compulsory, except those registered under Table A—Appointment under Table A—Under Companies Act, 1879—Under Companies Clauses Consolidation Act, 1845—By Board of Trade—Accounts of Life Assurance Companies need not be Audited—Appointment of Auditors under Friendly Societies Act, 1875—Under Industrial and Provident Societies Act, 1876 — Auditors occasionally appointed to guard special interests.

THE Companies Act, 1862, does not make it compulsory upon Companies registered under that Act to have Auditors, but in the first Schedule appended to that Act (usually known as Table A), which contains a number of regulations applicable to Companies which do not possess their own Articles of Association, it is laid down that once at least in every year the Accounts of these Companies shall be examined, and the correctness of the Balance Sheet ascertained by one or more Auditors.

Not compulsory by Companies Act, 1862, to have Auditors unless registered under Table A.

These Auditors are, in the first instance, to be appointed by the Directors, and they remain in office until the first General Meeting of the Shareholders, when they retire, but are immediately eligible for re-election by the Shareholders, in whose hands the

right of election of the Auditors thenceforward
rests.

Appointment
of Auditors
under Table A. Should a casual vacancy occur in the office of
Auditor, it is the duty of the Directors to forthwith
summon an Extraordinary General Meeting for the
purpose of supplying the same, and should neither
the Directors nor the Shareholders make any
appointment of Auditors, the Board of Trade may,
on the application of not less than five members of
the Company, appoint an Auditor for the current
year, and fix the remuneration to be paid to him by
the Company.

The Sections (83—94) of Table A which especially refer to the Auditors, are set forth in detail
hereafter, as are also the five preceding Sections
(78—82), which prescribe what Accounts have to
be kept by the Directors.

Banking Com-
panies regis-
tered under
Companies
Act, 1879,
obliged to
have Auditors. The Companies Act, 1879, which received the
royal assent on the 15th August of that year, has
made it compulsory upon every Banking Company
registered since that date as a limited Company to
have its Accounts examined by one or more Auditors, who are to be elected annually by the Company
in General Meeting.   An Auditor, on quitting office,
is at once eligible for re-election.

If any casual vacancy should occur, the surviving
Auditor or Auditors may act alone, but should there
be no surviving Auditor the Directors have to forthwith call an Extraordinary General Meeting for the
purpose of supplying the vacancy or vacancies.

Companies
Act, 1862,
appointment
of Auditors. When Companies registered under the Act of
1862 have Articles of Association, the Sections in

them which refer to the Auditor vary, as a rule, very little from the Sections in Table A already referred to.

The first Auditors are usually appointed by the Directors, and they remain in office until the first Meeting of the Shareholders, when they retire, but being eligible for re-election are, as a rule, continued in their appointments.

The custom of electing the same Auditors annually is a very sensible one. It is a great mistake to change the Auditors as long as the Shareholders are satisfied they do their duty properly. The longer an Auditor is in office the more familiar he becomes with the business of the Company, and consequently the more likely to detect any inaccuracies in the accounts, either accidental or intentional. *Advantages of re-electing retiring Auditors.*

When a Company has been incorporated by special Act of Parliament, such Act is incorporated with the Companies Clauses Consolidation Act, 1845 (8 Vict. cap. 16), whose clauses and provisions, save so far as they are expressly varied or excepted by the private Act, apply to the Company incorporated by such Act, and to the undertaking for carrying on which such Company has been incorporated, so far as the same are applicable thereto respectively; and such clauses and provisions, as well as the clauses and provisions of every other Act which are incorporated with the private Act, form part of such Act, and are construed together therewith as forming one Act. *Companies incorporated by special Acts subject to Companies Clauses Consolidation Act, 1845.*

With respect to the appointment of Auditors of Companies incorporated by special Act of Parlia- *Appointment of Auditors.*

ment, it is enacted by the Companies Clauses Consolidation Act, 1845, that, unless by the special Act, Auditors are directed to be appointed otherwise than by the Company, the Shareholders present, personally or by proxy, shall, at the first Ordinary Meeting after the passing of the special Act, elect the prescribed number of Auditors, and if no number is prescribed, two Auditors; and at the first Ordinary Meeting of the Company in each year thereafter the Company shall elect an Auditor to supply the place of the one retiring from office.

An Auditor once elected, unless he be removed or is disqualified or resigns, continues to be an Auditor until another is elected in his stead.

Qualification.

Not allowed to hold any other office.

Where no qualification is prescribed by the special Act, every Auditor is obliged to hold at least one share in the undertaking, but he is not allowed to hold any office in the Company, or be in any other manner interested in its concerns, except as a Shareholder.

Mode of re-election.

One of the Auditors (to be determined in the first instance by Ballot among themselves, unless they otherwise agree, and afterwards by seniority) goes out of office at the first Ordinary Meeting in each year, but he is at once eligible for re-election, and after any such re-election he is, with respect to the going out of office by rotation, deemed a new Auditor.

Should a vacancy occur among the Auditors during the current year, then, at any General Meeting of the Company, the vacancy may, if the Company think fit, be supplied by election of the Shareholders.

If at any meeting at which an election of Auditors ought to take place the prescribed quorum are not present within an hour appointed for the meeting, no election of Auditors shall be made, and the meeting stands adjourned to the following day at the same time and place ; and if at such adjourned meeting the prescribed quorum are not present within an hour from the time appointed for the meeting, the existing Auditors shall continue to act until new Auditors are appointed at the first Ordinary Meeting held in the following year.

With reference to the appointment of Auditors to Railway Companies, the Regulation of Railways Act, 1868, enacts that the Sections in the Companies Clauses Consolidation Act, 1845, which makes it necessary for an Auditor to hold at least one share shall not apply, and consequently their Auditors need not be Shareholders. *Auditors of Railway Companies need not be Shareholders.*

The Regulation of Railways Act, 1868, also enacts that the Board of Trade may, upon application made in pursuance of a resolution passed at a meeting of the Directors, or at a General Meeting of the Company, appoint an Auditor in addition to the Auditors of such Company, and it shall not be necessary for any such Auditor to be a Shareholder in the Company. *Board of Trade may appoint Auditors to Railway Companies.*

Under the Metropolis Waterworks Act, 1871, an Auditor is appointed by, and is removable by, the Board of Trade (Local Government Board), whose duty it is to Audit the Accounts of the Companies once in every half year. This Auditor is usually known as the Government Auditor, and performs *Auditor appointed by Board of Trade under Metropolis Waterworks Act, 1871* his duties independently of the Auditors appointed by the Shareholders.

Life Assurance Companies Act, 1870, does not provide for the appointment of Auditors. The Life Assurance Companies Act, 1870, which enacts that the Accounts of all Life Assurance Companies shall be deposited annually with the Board of Trade, does not provide that such Accounts shall be submitted to any Auditors. This was certainly a grave omission, and will no doubt be rectified in a future Act, as there is no class of Company which so imperatively demands a strict investigation of its Accounts. It is true that nearly all Life Insurance Companies have Auditors, but their names show that their qualification for these important appointments is less considered than the fact of their being men of position and influence.

Auditors of Friendly Societies. The Friendly Societies Act, 1875 (38 and 39 Vict., cap. 60), enacts that all Societies registered under this Act shall submit their Accounts for audit either to one of the Public Auditors referred to below, or to two or more Auditors appointed by the Society; but it does not lay down any rule as to their mode of election, beyond stating they shall be appointed as the Rules of each particular Society provide. The Treasury may from time to time appoint Public Auditors for the purposes of this Act, but it is optional with the Societies whether they employ any of these Public Auditors, or choose others to fill the appointments.

Auditors of Industrial and Provident Societies. The Industrial and Provident Societies Act, 1876 (39 and 40 Vict., cap. 45), prescribes that the Accounts of all Societies registered under this Act shall be Audited, and the regulations respecting the Auditors are almost identical with those of the Friendly Societies Act.

Although many professional accountants and others have been appointed by the Treasury Public Auditors under these Acts, the Societies have not hitherto taken advantage of these appointments, and seem to prefer Auditors chosen out of their numbers.

In a few Companies, Auditors are appointed to look after the interests of a particular class or section of those concerned in their welfare. *Auditors occasionally appointed to guard special interests.*

For instance, some Insurance Companies have Auditors for the Assured as well as for the Assurers or Shareholders. Occasionally the Debenture Holders of a Company have their own Auditor, as have also the Preference Shareholders.

This is, however, exceptional; in nearly all Companies the Auditors are the representatives of the general body of the Shareholders.

CHAPTER III.

SECTIONS OF THE STATUTES RELATING TO THE BOOKS, ACCOUNTS, AND AUDITORS OF JOINT STOCK COMPANIES AND FRIENDLY AND INDUSTRIAL AND PROVIDENT SOCIETIES.

The Companies Act, 1862—The Companies Act, 1879—The Companies Act, 1880—The Companies Clauses Consolidation Act, 1845—The Companies Clauses Consolidation Act, 1862 —The Railway Companies Securities Act, 1866—The Railway Companies Act, 1867—The Regulation of Railways Act, 1868—The Gasworks Clauses Act, 1847—The Gasworks Clauses Act, 1871—The Waterworks Clauses Act, 1847—The Metropolis Water Act, 1852—The Metropolis Water Act, 1871—The Life Assurance Companies Act, 1870—The Friendly Societies Act, 1875—The Friendly Societies Amendment Act, 1876—The Industrial and Provident Societies Act, 1876—The Falsification of Accounts Act, 1875.

Auditor should be acquainted with Acts of Parliament relating to Company.

As it is very necessary that every one holding an office of a public nature should clearly understand his legal responsibilities, an Auditor should be acquainted with the Acts of Parliament under which his appointment is made.

It is of course desirable he should be familiar with all the Acts regulating the Company or Society of which he is the Auditor, and special attention should be given to those sections relating to the Books and Accounts, and to the appointment and duties of the Auditors.

When a Company has been incorporated by Special Act of Parliament, or if registered under the Companies Act, 1862, has Articles of Association, the Auditor should be provided with a copy of the Private Act or the Articles of Association, and these should be read in conjunction with the Public Acts as explained in the first chapter.

The present chapter contains the sections of the Public Acts having reference to the books, accounts, and the appointment and duties of Auditors. The Acts of Parliament from which they are taken do not follow in chronological order, but for convenient reference are so arranged that the Acts referring to the same class of Companies will be found together.

The Companies Act, 1862.
(25 & 26 Vict., c. 89.)
[7th August, 1862.]

1. This Act may be cited for all Purposes as " The Companies Act, 1862." Short Title.

3. For the Purposes of this Act a Company that carries on the Business of Insurance in common with any other Business or Businesses shall be deemed to be an Insurance Company. Definition of Insurance Company.

15. In the Case of a Company limited by Shares, if the Memorandum of Association is not accompanied by Articles of Association, or in so far as the Articles do not exclude or modify the Regulations contained in the Table marked A. in the First Schedule hereto, the last-mentioned Regulations shall, so far as the same are applicable, be deemed to be the Regulations of the Company in the same Manner and to the Application of Table A.

same Extent as if they had been inserted in Articles of Association and the Articles had been duly registered.

Register of Members.

25. Every Company under this Act shall cause to be kept in one or more Books a Register of its Members, and there shall be entered therein the following Particulars :

(1.) The Names and Addresses and the Occupations, if any, of the Members of the Company, with the addition, in the Case of a Company having a Capital divided into Shares, of a Statement of the Shares held by each Member, distinguishing each Share by its Number; and of the Amount paid or agreed to be considered as paid on the Shares of each Member.

(2.) The Date at which the Name of any Person was entered in the Register as a Member.

(3.) The Date at which any Person ceased to be a Member.

Annual List of Members.

26. Every Company under this Act, and having a Capital divided into Shares, shall make, once at least in every Year, a List of all Persons who, on the Fourteenth Day succeeding the Day on which the Ordinary General Meeting, or if there is more than One Ordinary Meeting in each Year, the First of such Ordinary General Meetings is held, are Members of the Company ; and such List shall state the Names, Addresses, and Occupations of all the Members therein mentioned, and the Number of Shares held by each of them, and shall contain a Summary specifying the following Particulars :

(1.) The Amount of the Capital of the Company, and the Number of Shares into which it is divided :

(2.) The Number of Shares taken from the Commencement of the Company up to the Date of the Summary :

(3.) The Amount of Calls made on each Share :

(4.) The total Amount of Calls received :

(5.) The total Amount of Calls unpaid :

(6.) The total Amount of Shares forfeited :

(7.) The Names, Addresses, and Occupations of the Persons who have ceased to be Members since the last List was made, and the Number of Shares held by each of them.

The above List and Summary shall be contained in a separate Part of the Register, and shall be completed within Seven Days after such Fourteenth Day as is mentioned in this Section, and a Copy shall forthwith be forwarded to the Registrar of Joint Stock Companies.

30. No Notice of any Trust, expressed, implied, or constructive, shall be entered on the Register, or be receivable by the Registrar, in the Case of Companies under this Act, and registered in *England* or *Ireland*. *Entry of Trusts on Register.*

43. Every Limited Company under this Act shall keep a Register of all Mortgages and Charges specifically affecting Property of the Company, and shall enter in such Register in respect of each Mortgage or Charge a short Description of the Property mortgaged or charged, the Amount of Charge created, and the Names of the Mortgagees or Persons enti- *Register of Mortgages.*

tled to such Charge: If any Property of the Company is Mortgaged or Charged without such Entry as aforesaid being made, every Director, Manager, or other Officer of the Company who knowingly and wilfully authorises or permits the Omission of such Entry shall incur a Penalty not exceeding Fifty Pounds:

List of Directors to be sent to Registrar.

45. Every Company under this Act, and not having a Capital divided into Shares, shall keep at its Registered Office a Register containing the Names and Addresses and the Occupations of its Directors or Managers, and shall send to the Registrar of Joint Stock Companies a Copy of such Register, and shall from Time to Time notify to the Registrar any change that takes place in such Directors or Managers.

General Meeting of Company.

49. A General Meeting of every Company under this Act shall be held once at the least in every Year.

Evidence of Proceedings at Meetings.

67. Every Company under this Act shall cause Minutes of all Resolutions and Proceedings of General Meetings of the Company, and of the Directors or Managers of the Company in Cases where there are Directors or Managers, to be duly entered in Books to be from Time to Time provided for the Purpose; and any such Minute as aforesaid, if purporting to be signed by the Chairman of the Meeting at which such Resolutions were passed or Proceedings had, or by the Chairman of the next succeeding Meeting, shall be received as Evidence in all legal Proceedings.

FIRST SCHEDULE.

TABLE A.—REGULATIONS FOR MANAGEMENT OF A COMPANY LIMITED BY SHARES.

Dividends.

(72.) The Directors may, with the Sanction of the Company in General Meeting, declare a Dividend to be paid to the Members in proportion to their Shares.

(73.) No Dividend shall be payable except out of the Profits arising from the Business of the Company.

(74.) The Directors may, before recommending any Dividend, set aside out of the Profits of the Company such Sum as they think proper as a Reserved Fund to meet Contingencies, or for equalising Dividends, or for repairing or maintaining the Works connected with the Business of the Company, or any Part thereof; and the Directors may invest the Sum so set apart as a reserved Fund upon such Securities as they may select.

(77.) No Dividend shall bear Interest as against the Company.

Accounts.

(78.) The Directors shall cause true Accounts to be kept,

> Of the Stock in Trade of the Company ;
>
> Of the Sums of Money received and expended by the Company and the Matter in respect of which such Receipt and Expenditure takes place ; and,
>
> Of the Credits and Liabilities of the Company :

The Books of Account shall be kept at the registered Office of the Company, and, subject to any reasonable Restrictions as to the Time and Manner of inspecting the same that may be imposed by the Company in General Meeting, shall be open to the Inspection of the Members during the Hours of Business.

(79.) Once at the least in every Year the Directors shall lay before the Company in General Meeting a Statement of the Income and Expenditure for the past Year, made up to a date not more than Three Months before such Meeting.

(80.) The Statement so made shall show, arranged under the most convenient Heads, the Amount of gross Income, distinguishing the several sources from which it has been derived, and the Amount of gross Expenditure, distinguishing the Expense of the Establishment, Salaries, and other like Matters : Every Item of Expenditure fairly chargeable against the Year's Income shall be brought into account, so that a just Balance of Profit and Loss may be laid before the Meeting ; and in Cases where any Item of Expenditure which may in fairness be distributed over several Years has been incurred in any One Year the whole amount of such Item shall be stated, with the Addition of the Reasons why only a Portion of such Expenditure is charged against the Income of the Year.

(81.) A Balance Sheet shall be made out in every Year, and laid before the Company in General Meeting, and such Balance Sheet shall contain a Summary of the Property and Liabilities of the

Company arranged under the Heads appearing in the Form annexed to this Table, or as near thereto as Circumstances admit.

(82.) A printed Copy of such Balance Sheet shall, Seven Days previously to such Meeting, be served on every Member in the Manner in which Notices are herein-after directed to be served.

Audit.

(83.) Once at the least in every Year the Accounts of the Company shall be examined, and the Correctness of the Balance Sheet ascertained, by one or more Auditor or Auditors.

(84.) The First Auditors shall be appointed by the Directors: Subsequent Auditors shall be appointed by the Company in General Meeting.

(85.) If one Auditor only is appointed, all the Provisions herein contained relating to Auditors shall apply to him.

(86.) The Auditors may be Members of the Company; but no Person is eligible as an Auditor who is interested otherwise than as a Member in any Transaction of the Company; and no Director or other Officer of the Company is eligible during his continuance in Office.

(87.) The Election of Auditors shall be made by the Company at their Ordinary Meeting in each Year.

(88.) The Remuneration of the First Auditors shall be fixed by the Directors; that of subsequent Auditors shall be fixed by the Company in General Meeting.

(89.) Any Auditor shall be re-eligible on his quitting Office.

(90.) If any casual Vacancy occurs in the Office of any Auditor appointed by the Company, the Directors shall forthwith call an Extraordinary General Meeting for the Purpose of supplying the same.

(91.) If no Election of Auditors is made in manner aforesaid the Board of Trade may, on the Application of not less than Five Members of the Company, appoint an Auditor for the current Year, and fix the Remuneration to be paid to him by the Company for his Services.

(92.) Every Auditor shall be supplied with a Copy of the Balance Sheet, and it shall be his Duty to examine the same, with the Accounts and Vouchers relating thereto.

(93.) Every Auditor shall have a List delivered to him of all Books kept by the Company, and shall, at all reasonable Times, have Access to the Books and Accounts of the Company. He may, at the Expense of the Company, employ Accountants or other Persons to assist him in investigating such Accounts, and he may in relation to such Accounts examine the Directors or any other Officer of the Company.

(94.) The Auditors shall make a Report to the Members upon the Balance Sheet and Accounts, and in every such Report they shall state whether in their opinion the Balance Sheet is a full and fair Balance Sheet, containing the Particulars required by these Regulations, and properly drawn up so as to exhibit a true and correct View of the State of

the Company's Affairs; and in case they have called
for Explanations or Information from the Directors,
whether such Explanations or Information have
been given by the Directors, and whether they have
been satisfactory; and such Report shall be read,
together with the Report of the Directors, at the
Ordinary Meeting.

SECOND SCHEDULE.

FORM B.—MEMORANDUM AND ARTICLES OF ASSOCIATION OF A COMPANY LIMITED BY GUARANTEE, AND NOT HAVING A CAPITAL DIVIDED INTO SHARES.

Accounts.

(29.) The Accounts of the Company shall be
Audited by a Committee of Five Members, to be
called the Audit Committee.

(30.) The First Audit Committee shall be nomi-
nated by the Directors out of the Body of Members.

(31.) Subsequent Audit Committees shall be nomi-
nated by the Members at the Ordinary General Meeting in each Year.

(32.) The Audit Committee shall be supplied with
a Copy of the Balance Sheet, and it shall be their
Duty to examine the same with the Accounts and
Vouchers relating thereto.

(33.) The Audit Committee shall have a List
delivered to them of all Books kept by the Company,
and they shall at all reasonable Times have Access
to the Books and Accounts of the Company: They
may, at the Expense of the Company, employ Accountants or other Persons to assist them in investi-

gating such Accounts, and they may in relation to such Accounts examine the Directors or any other Officer of the Company.

(34.) The Audit Committee shall make a Report to the Members upon the Balance Sheet and Accounts, and in every such Report they shall state whether in their Opinion the Balance Sheet is a full and fair Balance Sheet, containing the Particulars required by these Regulations of the Company, and properly drawn up, so as to exhibit a true and correct View of the State of the Company's Affairs, and in case they have called for Explanation or Information from the Directors, whether such Explanations or Information have been given by the Directors, and whether they have been satisfactory, and such Report shall be read together with the Report of the Directors at the Ordinary Meeting.

The Companies Act, 1879.
(42 & 43 Vict., c. 76.)

[15th August, 1879.]

Short Title.   1. This Act may be cited as the Companies Act, 1879.

Act not to apply to Bank of England.   2. This Act shall not apply to the Bank of England.

Act to be construed with 25 & 26 Vict., c. 89, 30 & 31 Vict., c. 131, and 40 & 41 Vict., c. 26.   3. This Act shall, so far as is consistent with the tenor thereof, be construed as one with the Companies Acts, 1862, 1867, and 1877, and those Acts together with this Act may be referred to as the Companies Acts, 1862 to 1879.

7. (1.) Once at the least in every year the Ac- counts of every Banking Company registered after the passing of this Act as a Limited Company shall be examined by an Auditor or Auditors, who shall be elected Annually by the Company in General Meeting.

(2.) A Director or Officer of the Company shall not be capable of being elected Auditor of such Company.

(3.) An Auditor on quitting office shall be re-eligible.

(4.) If any casual vacancy occurs in the office of any Auditor, the surviving Auditor or Auditors (if any) may act, but if there is no surviving Auditor, the Directors shall forthwith call an Extraordinary General Meeting for the purpose of supplying the vacancy or vacancies in the Auditorship.

(5.) Every Auditor shall have a List delivered to him of all Books kept by the Company, and shall at all reasonable times have Access to the Books and Accounts of the Company; and any Auditor may, in relation to such Books and Accounts, examine the Directors or any other Officer of the Company: Provided that if a Banking Company has branch Banks beyond the limits of Europe, it shall be sufficient if the Auditor is allowed access to such copies of and extracts from the Books and Accounts of any such branch as may have been transmitted to the head office of the Banking Company in the United Kingdom.

(6.) The Auditor or Auditors shall make a Report to the Members on the Accounts examined by him or them, and on every Balance Sheet laid before the Company in General Meeting during his or their tenure of office; and in every such Report shall state whether, in his or their opinion, the Balance Sheet referred to in the Report is a full and fair Balance Sheet, properly drawn up, so as to exhibit a true and correct view of the state of the Company's affairs, as shown by the Books of the Company; and such Report shall be read before the Company in General Meeting.

(7.) The remuneration of the Auditor or Auditors shall be fixed by the General Meeting appointing such Auditor or Auditors, and shall be paid by the Company.

Signature of Balance Sheet 8. Every Balance Sheet submitted to the Annual or other Meeting of the Members of every Banking Company registered after the passing of this Act as a Limited Company shall be signed by the Auditor or Auditors, and by the Secretary or Manager (if any), and by the Directors of the Company, or three of such Directors at the least.

THE COMPANIES ACT, 1880.
(43 Vict., c. 19.)

[24th March, 1880.]

Short Title. 1. This Act may be cited for all purposes as the Companies Act, 1880.

Construction of Acts.

25 & 26 Vict., c. 89, 30 & 31 Vict., c. 131, 2. This Act shall, so far as is consistent with the tenor thereof, be construed as one with the Companies Acts, 1862, 1867, 1877, and 1879, and the

said Acts and this Act may be referred to as the _{40 & 41 Vict., c. 26,} Companies Acts, 1862 to 1880. _{42 & 43 Vict., c. 76.}

3. When any Company has accumulated a sum of Accumulated profits may be undivided profits, which with the consent of the returned to Shareholders may be distributed among the Share-holders in reduction of paid-up holders in the form of a Dividend or Bonus, it shall Capital. be lawful for the Company, by Special Resolution, to return the same, or any part thereof, to the Share-holders in reduction of the paid-up capital of the Company, the unpaid capital being thereby increased by a similar amount. The powers vested in the Directors of making calls upon the Shareholders in respect of moneys unpaid upon their shares shall extend to the amount of the unpaid capital as augmented by such reduction.

4. No such Special Resolution as aforesaid shall No Resolution to take effect take effect until a Memorandum, showing the par- till particulars have been ticulars required by law in the case of a reduction registered. of capital by order of the Court, shall have been produced to and registered by the Registrar of Joint Stock Companies.

5. Upon any reduction of paid-up capital made Power to any Shareholder in pursuance of this Act, it shall be lawful for any within one month after Shareholder, or for any one or more of several Joint passing of Resolution to Shareholders, within one month after the passing of require Com-pany to retain the Special Resolution for such reduction, to require moneys paid the Company to retain, and the Company shall upon Shares held by such retain accordingly, the whole of the moneys actually person. paid upon the shares held by such person, either alone or jointly with any other person or persons, and which, in consequence of such reduction, would otherwise be returned to him or them, and thereupon

the shares in respect of which the said moneys shall be so retained shall, in regard to the payment of dividends thereon, be deemed to be paid up to the same extent only as the shares on which payment as aforesaid has been accepted by the Shareholders in reduction of their paid-up capital, and the Company shall invest and keep invested the moneys so retained in such securities authorised for investment by Trustees as the Company shall determine, and upon the money so invested, or upon so much thereof as from time to time exceeds the amount of calls subsequently made upon the shares in respect of which such moneys shall have been retained, the Company shall pay such interest as shall be received by them from time to time on such securities, and the amount so retained and invested shall be held to represent the future calls which may be made to replace the capital so reduced on those shares, whether the amount obtained on sale of the whole or such proportion thereof as represents the amount of any call when made, produces more or less than the amount of such call.

6. From and after such reduction of capital the Company shall specify in the annual lists of members, to be made by them in pursuance of the twenty-sixth Section of the Companies Act, 1862, the amounts which any of the Shareholders of the Company shall have required the Company to retain, and the Company shall have retained accordingly, in pursuance of the fifth Section of this Act, and the Company shall also specify in the statements of account laid before any general meeting of the Com-

Company to specify amounts which Shareholders have required them to retain under s. 5; also to specify amounts of profits returned to Shareholders. 25 & 26 Vict., c. 89.

pany the amount of the undivided profits of the Company which shall have been returned to the Shareholders in reduction of the paid-up capital of the Company under this Act.

THE COMPANIES CLAUSES CONSOLIDATION ACT, 1845.
(8 Vict., c. 16.)

[8th May, 1845.]

This Act shall apply to every Joint Stock Company which shall by any Act which shall hereafter be passed be incorporated for the Purpose of carrying on any Undertaking, and this Act shall be incorporated with such Act : and all the Clauses and Provisions of this Act, save so far as they shall be expressly varied or excepted by any such Act, shall apply to the Company which shall be incorporated by such Act, and to the Undertaking for carrying on which such Company shall be incorporated, so far as the same shall be applicable thereto respectively; and such Clauses and Provisions, as well as the Clauses and Provisions of every other Act which shall be incorporated with such Act, shall, save as aforesaid, form Part of such Act, and be construed together therewith as forming One Act. *(margin: Act to apply to all Companies incorporated by Acts hereafter to be passed.)*

9. The Company shall keep a Book to be called the "Register of Shareholders;" and in such Book shall be fairly and distinctly entered, from Time to Time, the Names of the several Corporations, and the Names and Additions of the several Persons entitled to Shares in the Company, together with the Number *(margin: Register of Shareholders.)*

of Shares to which such Shareholders shall be respectively entitled, distinguishing each Share by its Number, and the Amount of the Subscriptions paid on such Shares, and the Surnames or Corporate Names of the said Shareholders shall be placed in alphabetical Order; and such Book shall be authenticated by the Common Seal of the Company being affixed thereto; and such Authentication shall take place at the First Ordinary Meeting, or at the next subsequent Meeting of the Company, and so from Time to Time at each Ordinary Meeting of the Company.

Addresses of Shareholders. 10. In addition to the said Register of Shareholders, the Company shall provide a Book, to be called the " Shareholders Address Book," in which the Secretary shall from Time to Time enter in alphabetical Order the Corporate Names and Places of Business of the several Shareholders of the Company, being Corporations, and the Surnames of the several other Shareholders, with their respective Christian Names, Places of Abode, and Descriptions, so far as the same shall be known to the Company.

Register of Mortgages and Bonds. 45. A Register of Mortgages and Bonds shall be kept by the Secretary, and within Fourteen Days after the Date of any such Mortgage or Bond an Entry or Memorial, specifying the Number and Date of such Mortgage or Bond, and the sums secured thereby, and the Names of the Parties thereto, with their proper Additions, shall be made in such Register.

Payment of Interest on Moneys borrowed. 48. The Interest of the Money borrowed upon any such Mortgage or Bond shall be paid at the

Periods appointed in such Mortgage or Bond, and if no Period be appointed half-yearly, to the several Parties entitled thereto, and in preference to any Dividends payable to the Shareholders of the Company.

61. It shall be lawful for the Company from Time to Time, with the Consent of Three Fifths of the Votes of the Shareholders present in Person or by Proxy at any General Meeting of the Company, when due Notice for that Purpose shall have been given, to convert or consolidate all or any Part of the Shares then existing in the Capital of the Company, and in respect whereof the whole Money subscribed shall have been paid up, into a General Capital Stock, to be divided amongst the Shareholders according to their respective Interests therein.

Power to consolidate Shares into Stock.

63. The Company shall from Time to Time cause the Names of the several Parties who may be interested in any such Stock as aforesaid, with the Amount of the Interest therein possessed by them respectively, to be entered in a Book to be kept for the Purpose, and to be called " The Register of Holders of Consolidated Stock."

Register of Stock.

And with respect to the Appointment and Duties of Auditors, be it enacted as follows :

101. Except where by the Special Act Auditors shall be directed to be appointed otherwise than by the Company, the Company shall, at the First Ordinary Meeting after the passing of the Special Act, elect the prescribed Number of Auditors, and if no Number is prescribed Two Auditors, in like Manner as is provided for the Election of Directors;

Election of Auditors.

3

and at the First Ordinary Meeting of the Company in each Year thereafter the Company shall in like Manner elect an Auditor to supply the Place of the Auditor then retiring from Office, according to the Provision hereinafter contained; and every Auditor elected as hereinbefore provided, being neither removed nor disqualified nor having resigned, shall continue to be an Auditor until another be elected in his Stead.

Qualification of Auditors.

102. Where no other Qualification shall be prescribed by the Special Act, every Auditor shall have at least One Share in the Undertaking; and he shall not hold any Office in the Company, nor be in any other Manner interested in its Concerns, except as a Shareholder.

Rotation of Auditors.

103. One of such Auditors (to be determined in the first instance by Ballot between themselves, unless they shall otherwise agree, and afterwards by Seniority) shall go out of office at the First Ordinary Meeting in each Year; but the Auditor so going out shall be immediately re-eligible, and after any such Re-election shall, with respect to the going out of Office by Rotation, be deemed a new Auditor.

Vacancies in Office of Auditor.

104. If any Vacancy take place among the Auditors in the course of the current Year, then at any General Meeting of the Company the Vacancy may, if the Company think fit, be supplied by Election of the Shareholders.

Failure of Meeting to elect Auditor.

105. The Provision of this Act respecting the Failure of an Ordinary Meeting at which Directors ought to be chosen shall apply, *mutatis mutandis*, to

any Ordinary Meeting at which an Auditor ought to be appointed.

106. The Directors shall deliver to such Auditors the half-yearly or other periodical Accounts and Balance Sheet, Fourteen Days at the least before the ensuing Ordinary Meeting at which the same are required to be produced to the Shareholders as hereinafter provided. *Delivery of Balance Sheet, &c., by Directors to Auditors.*

107. It shall be the Duty of such Auditors to receive from the Directors the half-yearly or other periodical Accounts and Balance Sheet required to be presented to the Shareholders, and to examine the same. *Duty of Auditors.*

108. It shall be lawful for the Auditors to employ such Accountants and other Persons as they may think proper, at the Expense of the Company, and they shall either make a Special Report on the said Accounts, or simply confirm the same ; and such Report or Confirmation shall be read, together with the Report of the Directors, at the Ordinary Meeting. *Powers of Auditors.*

And with respect to the keeping of Accounts be it enacted as follows :

115. The Directors shall cause full and true Accounts to be kept of all Sums of Money received or expended on account of the Company by the Directors and all Persons employed by or under them, and of the Matters and Things for which such Sums of Money shall have been received or disbursed and paid. *Accounts to be kept.*

116. The Books of the Company shall be balanced at the prescribed Periods, and, if no Periods be prescribed, Fourteen Days at least before each Ordinary *Books to be balanced.*

Meeting; and forthwith on the Books being so balanced an exact Balance Sheet shall be made up, which shall exhibit a true Statement of the Capital Stock, Credits, and Property of every Description belonging to the Company, and the Debts due by the Company at the Date of making such Balance Sheet, and a distinct View of the Profit or Loss which shall have arisen on the Transactions of the Company in the course of the preceding Half Year; and previously to each Ordinary Meeting such Balance Sheet shall be examined by the Directors, or any three of their Number, and shall be signed by the Chairman or Deputy Chairman of the Directors.

Balance Sheet to be produced at the Meeting.

118. The Directors shall produce to the Shareholders assembled at such Ordinary Meeting the said Balance Sheet, applicable to the period immediately preceding such Meeting, together with the Report of the Auditors thereon, as hereinbefore provided.

And with respect to the making of Dividends, be it enacted as follows:

Previously to Declaration of Dividends a Scheme to be prepared.

120. Previously to every Ordinary Meeting at which a Dividend is intended to be declared the Directors shall cause a Scheme to be prepared, showing the Profits, if any, of the Company for the Period current since the preceding Ordinary Meeting at which a Dividend was declared, and apportioning the same, or so much thereof as they may consider applicable to the Purposes of Dividend, among the Shareholders, according to the Shares held by them respectively, the Amount paid thereon,

and the Periods during which the same may have been paid, and shall exhibit such Scheme at such Ordinary Meeting, and at such Meeting a Dividend may be declared according to such Scheme.

121. The Company shall not make any Dividend whereby their Capital Stock will be in any Degree reduced: Provided always, that the Word "Dividend" shall not be construed to apply to a Return of any Portion of the Capital Stock, with the Consent of all the Mortgagees and Bond Creditors of the Company, due Notice being given for that Purpose at an Extraordinary Meeting to be convened for that Object. *Dividend not to be made so as to reduce Capital.*

122. Before apportioning the Profits to be divided among the Shareholders the Directors may, if they think fit, set aside thereout such Sum as they may think proper to meet Contingencies, or for enlarging, repairing, or improving the Works connected with the Undertaking, or any Part thereof, and may divide the Balance only among the Shareholders. *Power to Directors to set apart a Fund for Contingencies.*

123. No Dividends shall be paid in respect of any Share until all calls then due in respect of that and every other Share held by the Person to whom such Dividend may be payable shall have been paid. *Dividend not to be paid unless all Calls paid.*

THE COMPANIES CLAUSES ACT, 1863.
(26 & 27 Vict., c. 118).

[28th July, 1863.]

1. This Act may be cited as The Companies Clauses Act, 1863. *Short Title.*

Preference Shares to be entitled to Dividends only out of the Profits of each Year. 14. The Preference Shares or Preference Stock shall be entitled to the preferential Dividend or Interest assigned thereto, out of the Profits of each Year, in priority to the Ordinary Shares and Ordinary Stock of the Company; but if in any Year ending on the Day prescribed in the Special Act, and if no Day is prescribed, then on the Thirty-first Day of *December*, there are not Profits available for the Payment of the full Amount of preferential Dividend or Interest for that Year, no Part of the Deficiency shall be made good out of the Profits of any subsequent Year, or out of any other Funds of the Company.

Interest on Debenture Stock to be a primary Charge. 24. The Interest on Debenture Stock shall have Priority of Payment over all Dividends or Interest on any Shares or Stock of the Company, whether Ordinary, or Preference or guaranteed, and shall rank next to the Interest payable on the Mortgages or Bonds for the Time being of the Company legally granted before the Creation of such Stock; but the Holders of Debenture Stock shall not, as among themselves, be entitled to any Preference or Priority.

Debenture Stock to be registered. 28. The Company shall cause Entries of the Debenture Stock from Time to Time created to be made in a Register to be kept for that Purpose, wherein they shall enter the Names and Addresses of the several Persons and Corporations from Time to Time entitled to the Debenture Stock, with the respective Amounts of the Stock to which they are respectively entitled.

Separate Accounts of 33. Separate and distinct Accounts shall be kept by the Company, showing how much Money has been received for or on account of Debenture Stock, and how much Money borrowed or owing on Mortgage or Bond, or which they have power so to borrow, has been paid off by Debenture Stock, or raised thereby, instead of being borrowed on Mortgage or Bond. *Debenture Stock.*

THE RAILWAY COMPANIES SECURITIES ACT, 1866.
(29 & 30 Vict., c. 108.)
[10th August, 1866.]

1. This Act may be cited as the Railway Companies Securities Act, 1866. *Short Title.*

2. In this Act—

The Term " Railway " includes a Tramway authorised by Act of Parliament incorporating The Companies Clause Consolidation Act, 1845, but not any other Tramway : *Interpretation of Terms.*

The Term " Railway Company " includes every Company authorised by Act of Parliament to raise any Loan Capital for the Construction or Working of a Railway, or for any Purposes connected with the Conveyance by such Company of Traffic on a Railway, either alone or in conjunction with other Purposes :

The Term " Debenture Stock " includes Mortgage Preference Stock and Funded Debt, and any Stock or Shares representing Loan Capital of a Railway Company, by whatever Name called.

Half Years for Purposes of Act.

4. Half Years shall, for the purposes of this Act, be deemed to end on the Thirtieth Day of *June* and the Thirty-first Day of *December* ; and the First Half Year to which this Act applies shall be that ending on the Thirty-first Day of *December*, One thousand eight hundred and sixty-six ; but the Board of Trade, on the Application of any Railway Company, may (by Writing under the Hand of One of their Secretaries or Assistant Secretaries, which shall be registered by the Railway Company at the Office of the said Registrar) appoint, with respect to that Company, other Days for the ending of Half Years (including the First).

Loan Capital Accounts to be made half-yearly.

5. Within Fourteen Days after the End of each Half Year every Railway Company shall make an Account of their Loan Capital authorised to be raised and actually raised up to the End of that Half Year, specifying the Particulars described in the First Schedule to this Act, Part I (which Account for each Half Year is in this Act referred to as the Loan Capital Half-yearly Account).

Form of Half-yearly Account.

6. The Board of Trade may from Time to Time, by Notice published in the *London*, *Edinburgh*, and *Dublin* Gazettes, prescribe the Form in which the Loan Capital Half-yearly Account is to be made.

The First Schedule.

Part 1.—Particulars to be Specified in Loan Capital Half-yearly Account.

A. Every Half-yearly Account to show—

(1.) The Act or Acts of Parliament under the Powers of which the Company have contracted any

Mortgage or Bond Debt existing at the End of the Half Year, or have issued any Debenture Stock then existing, or the Act or Acts of Parliament by or under which any Mortgage or Bond Debt or Debenture Stock of the Company then existing has been confirmed, and the Act or Acts of Parliament under which the Company have any subsisting Power to contract any Mortgage or Bond Debt, or to issue any Debenture Stock (either on Fulfilment of any Condition or otherwise) :

(2.) The Amount or respective Amounts of Mortgage or Bond Debt or Debenture Stock thereby authorised or confirmed :

(3.) Whether or not by any such Act or Acts the obtaining of the Certificate of a Justice or Sheriff for any purpose, or the obtaining of the Assent of a Meeting of the Company, has been made a Condition precedent to the Exercise of the Power thereby conferred of borrowing on Mortgage or Bond, or of creating and issuing Debenture Stock :

(4.) The Date at which such Condition has been fulfilled :

(5.) The Amount or the aggregate Amount, under the Powers of such Act or Acts, actually borrowed up to the End of the Half Year on Mortgage or Bond (distinguishing them), and then being an existing Debt, and of Debenture Stock actually issued up to that Time and then existing :

(6.) The Amount or the aggregate Amount remaining to be borrowed.

B. The Second and every subsequent Half-yearly Account to show also—

(7.) The Items described in Paragraphs (2.) and
(5.) of this Part of the present Schedule for Two
consecutive Half Years, and the Increase or Decrease
of any of those Items in the Second of those Half
Years as compared with the First.

THE RAILWAY COMPANIES ACT, 1867.
(30 & 31 Vict., c. 127.)
[20th August, 1867.]

Short Title. 1. This Act may be cited as The Railway Companies Act, 1867.

Priority of Mortgages. 23. All Money borrowed or to be borrowed by a
Company on Mortgage or Bond or Debenture Stock,
under the Provisions of any Act authorising the
borrowing thereof shall have Priority against the
Company, and the Property from Time to Time of
the Company, over all other claims on account of
any Debts incurred or Engagements entered into by
them after the passing of this Act : Provided always,
that this Priority shall not affect any Claim against
the Company in respect of any Rentcharge granted
or to be granted by them in pursuance of The
Lands Clauses Consolidation Act, 1845, or The
Lands Clauses Consolidation Acts Amendment Act,
1860, or in respect of any Rent or Sum reserved by
or payable under any Lease granted or made to the
Company by any Person in pursuance of any Act
relating to the Company which is entitled to rank in
priority to, or *pari passu* with, the Interest or Dividends on the Mortgages, Bonds, and Debenture Stock.

Audit of Railway Accounts. 30. No Dividend shall be declared by a Company
until the Auditors have certified that the Half-yearly

Accounts proposed to be issued contain a full and true Statement of the financial Condition of the Company, and that the Dividend proposed to be declared on any Shares is *bonâ fide* due thereon after charging the Revenue of the Half Year with all Expenses which ought to be paid thereout in the Judgment of the Auditors; but if the Directors differ from the Judgment of the Auditors with respect to the Payment of any such Expenses out of the Revenue of the Half Year, such Difference shall, if the Directors desire it, be stated in the Report to the Shareholders, and the Company in General Meeting may decide thereon, subject to all the Provisions of the Law then existing, and such Decision shall for the Purposes of the Dividend be final and binding; but if no such Difference is stated or if no Decision is given on any such Difference, the judgment of the Auditors shall be final and binding; and the Auditors may examine the Books of the Company at all reasonable times, and may call for such further Accounts, and such Vouchers, Papers, and Information, as they think fit, and the Directors and Officers of the Company shall produce and give the same as far as they can, and the Auditors may refuse to certify as aforesaid until they have received the same; and the Auditors may at any Time add to their Certificate, or issue to the Shareholders independently at the Cost of the Company, any Statement respecting the financial Condition and Prospects of the Company which they think material for the Information of the Shareholders.

The Regulation of Railways Act, 1868.
(31 & 32 Vict., c. 119.)

[31st July, 1868.]

Short Title.
1. This Act may be cited as " The Regulation of Railways Act, 1868."

2. In this Act—

Interpretation of Terms.
The Term " Railway " means the Whole or any Portion of a Railway or Tramway, whether worked by Steam or otherwise.

1.—*Accounts, Audit, &c.*

Uniform Accounts, &c., to be kept.
3. Every incorporated Company, Seven Days at least before each ordinary half-yearly Meeting held after the Thirty-first Day of *December* One thousand eight hundred and sixty-eight, shall prepare and print, according to the Forms contained in the First Schedule to this Act, a Statement of Accounts and Balance Sheet for the last preceding Half Year, and the other Statements and Certificates required by the same Schedule, and an estimate of the proposed Expenditure out of Capital for the next ensuing Half Year, and such Statement of Accounts and Balance Sheet shall be the Statement of Accounts and Balance Sheet which are submitted to the Auditors of the Company. Every Company which makes default in complying with this Section shall be liable to a Penalty not exceeding Five Pounds for every day during which such Default continues. The Board of Trade with the Consent of a Company, may alter the said Forms as regards such Company for the Purpose of adapting them to the Circum-

stances of such Company, or of better carrying into effect the Objects of this Section.

4. Every Statement of Accounts, Balance Sheet, and Estimate of Expenditure, prepared as required by this Act, shall be signed by the Chairman or Deputy Chairman of the Directors and by the Accountant or other Officer in charge of the Accounts of the Company, and shall be preserved at the Company's principal Office. A printed Copy thereof shall be forwarded to the Board of Trade. *Accounts, &c., to be signed, and printed Copies distributed.*

5. If any Statement, Balance Sheet, Estimate, or Report which is required by this Act, is false in any Particular to the Knowledge of any Person who signs the same, such Person shall be liable, on Conviction thereof on Indictment, to Fine and Imprisonment, or on summary Conviction thereof to a Penalty not exceeding Fifty Pounds. *Penalty for falsifying Accounts, &c.*

11. Whenever, after the passing of this Act, Section One hundred and two of the Companies Clauses Consolidation Act, 1845, is incorporated in a Certificate or Special Act relating to a Railway Company, it shall be construed as if the Words, " where no Qualification shall be prescribed by the Special Act every Auditor shall have at least One Share in the Undertaking," were omitted therefrom; and so much of every Certificate and Special Act relating to a Railway Company, and in force at the passing of this Act, as incorporates that Portion of the said Section, and so much of any Special Act relating to a Railway Company, and so in force, as contains a like Provision, is hereby repealed. *Auditor not necessarily a Shareholder.*

Auditors of
Company, and
Appointment
of Auditor by
Board of
Trade.

12. With respect to the Auditors of the Company the following Provisions shall have Effect :

(1.) The Board of Trade may, upon Application made in pursuance of a Resolution passed at a Meeting of the Directors or at a General Meeting of the Company, appoint an Auditor in addition to the Auditors of such Company, and it shall not be necessary for any such Auditor to be a Shareholder in the Company.

(2.) The Company shall pay to such Auditor appointed by the Board of Trade such reasonable Remuneration as the Board of Trade may prescribe :

(3.) The Auditor so appointed shall have the same Duties and Powers as the Auditors of the Company, and shall report to the Company :

(4.) Where, in consequence of such Appointment of an Auditor or otherwise, there are Three or more Auditors, the Company may declare a Dividend if the Majority of such Auditors certify in manner required by Section Thirty of the Railway Companies Act, 1867, and the Railway Companies (*Scotland*) Act, 1867, respectively :

(5.) Where there is a Difference of Opinion among such Auditors, the Auditor who so differs shall issue to the Shareholders, at the Cost of the Company, such Statement respecting the Grounds on which he differs from his Colleagues, and respecting the Financial Condition and Prospects of the Company, as he thinks material for the Information of the Shareholders.

13. Any Company which in the Year immediately preceding has paid a Dividend on their Ordinary

Stock of not less than Three Pounds *per Centum* *per Annum* may, pursuant to the Resolution of an Extraordinary General Meeting, divide their paid-up Ordinary Stock into Two Classes, to be and to be called the one Preferred Ordinary Stock, and the other Deferred Ordinary Stock, and issue the same subject and according to the following Provisions,and with the following consequences; (that is to say,)

(1.) Preferred and Deferred Ordinary Stock shall be issued only in substitution for equal Amounts of paid-up Ordinary Stock, and by way of Division of Portions of Ordinary Stock into Two equal Parts:

(6.) As between Preferred Ordinary Stock and Deferred Ordinary Stock, Preferred Ordinary Stock shall bear a fixed maximum Dividend at the Rate of Six *per Centum per Annum:*

(7.) In respect of Dividend to the Extent of the Maximum aforesaid, Preferred Ordinary Stock shall at the Time of its Creation, and at all Times afterwards, have Priority over Deferred Ordinary Stock created or to be created, and shall rank *pari passu* with the undivided Ordinary Stock and the Ordinary Shares of the Company created or to be created; and in respect of Dividend, Preferred Ordinary Stock shall at all Times and to all Intents rank after all preference and guaranteed Stock and Shares of the Company created or to be created:

(8.) In each Year after all Holders of Preferred Ordinary Stock for the Time being issued have received in full the maximum Dividend aforesaid, all Holders of Deferred Ordinary Stock for the Time being issued shall, in respect of all Dividend exceeding that Maximum paid by the Company in that Year on Ordinary Stock and Shares, rank *pari passu* with the Holders of undivided Ordinary Stock and of Ordinary shares of the Company for the Time being issued:

(9.) If, nevertheless, in any Year ending on the Thirty-first Day of *December* there are not Profits available for Payment to all the Holders of Preferred Ordinary Stock of the maximum Dividend aforesaid, no Part of the Deficiency shall be made good out of the Profits of any subsequent Year, or out of any other Funds of the Company.

Extension of Scope of Railway Companies Powers Act, 1864.

38. The Railway Companies Powers Act, 1864, shall take effect and apply in the following Cases in the same Manner as if they were specified in Section Three of that Act; (that is to say,)

Where a Company desire to make new Provisions, or to alter any of the Provisions of their Special Act, or of the "Companies Clauses Consolidation Act, 1845," so far as it is incorporated therewith, with respect to all or any of the Matters following; namely.

(e.) The Appointment and Duties of Auditors.

THE GASWORKS CLAUSES ACT, 1847.
(10 Vict., c. 15.)

[23rd April, 1847.]

Special Act."

2. The Expression "the Special Act," used in this Act, shall be construed to mean any Act which

shall be hereafter passed authorising the Construction of Gasworks, and with which this Act shall be so incorporated as aforesaid; "the Undertaking" "The Undertaking." shall mean the Gasworks and the Works connected therewith by the Special Act authorised to be constructed; and the Expression "the Undertakers" "The Undertakers." shall mean the Persons by the Special Act authorised to construct the Gasworks.

4. In citing this Act in other Acts of Parliament Short Title of the Act. and in Legal Instruments, it shall be enough to use the Expression "The Gasworks Clauses Act, 1847."

30. The Profits of the Undertaking to be Profits of the Company limited. divided amongst the Undertakers in any Year shall not exceed the prescribed Rate, or where no Rate is prescribed, they shall not exceed the Rate of Ten Pounds in the Hundred by the Year on the paid-up Capital in the Undertaking, which in such Case shall be deemed the prescribed Rate, unless a larger Dividend be at any Time necessary to make up the Deficiency of any previous Dividend which shall have fallen short of the said yearly Rate.

31. If the clear Profits of the Undertaking in If Profits exceed the Amount limited Excess to be invested and form a reserved Fund. any Year amount to a larger Sum than is sufficient after making up the Deficiency in the Dividends of any previous Year as aforesaid, to make a Dividend at the prescribed Rate, the Excess beyond the Sum necessary for such Purpose shall from Time to Time be invested in Government or other Securities; and the Dividends and Interest arising from such Securities shall also be invested in the same or like Securities, in order that the same may accumulate at Compound Interest until the Fund so formed amounts

to the prescribed Sum, or if no Sum be prescribed, a Sum equal to One Tenth of the nominal Capital of the Undertakers, which Sum shall form a reserved Fund to answer any Deficiency which may at any Time happen in the Amount of divisible Profits, or to meet any extraordinary Claim or Demand which may at any Time arise against the Undertakers; and if such Fund be at any Time reduced, it may thereafter be again restored to the said Sum, and so from Time to Time as often as such Reduction shall happen.

Reserved Fund not to be resorted to unless to meet an extraordinary Claim.
32. Provided always, That no Sum of Money shall be taken from the said Fund for the Purpose of meeting any extraordinary Claim, unless it be first certified in *England* or *Ireland* by Two Justices, and in *Scotland* by the Sheriff, that the Sum so proposed to be taken is required for the Purpose of meeting an extraordinary Claim within the Meaning of this or the Special Act.

When Fund amounts to prescribed Sum, Interest to be applied to Purposes of the Undertaking.
33. When such Fund shall, by Accumulation or otherwise, amount to the prescribed Sum, or One Tenth of the nominal Capital of the Company, as the Case may be, the Interest and Dividends thereon shall no longer be invested, but shall be applied to any of the general Purposes of the Undertaking to which the Profits thereof are applicable.

If Profits are less than the prescribed Rate, a Sum may be taken from the reserved Fund to supply Deficiency.
34. If in any Year the Profits of the Undertaking divisible amongst the Undertakers shall not amount to the prescribed Rate, such a Sum may be taken from the reserved Fund as, with the actual divisible Profits of such Year, will enable the Undertakers to make a Dividend of the Amount aforesaid, and so

from Time to Time as often as the Occasion shall require.

38. And with respect to the yearly Receipt and Expenditure of the Undertakers, be it enacted, That the Undertakers shall, in each Year after they have begun to supply Gas under the Provisions of this or the Special Act, cause an Account in abstract to be prepared of the total Receipts and Expenditure of all Rents or Funds levied under the Powers of this or the Special Act for the Year preceding, under the several distinct Heads of Receipt and Expenditure, with a Statement of the Balance of such Account, duly audited and certified by the Chairman of the Undertakers, and also by the Auditors thereof, if any ; and a Copy of such annual Account, if the Gasworks be situated in *England* or *Ireland,* shall be transmitted, free of Charge, to the Clerk of the Peace for the County in which the Gasworks are situate, and if the Gasworks be situated in *Scotland,* such Copy shall be transmitted, free of Charge as aforesaid, to the Sheriff Clerk of such County, and such Transmission shall be made on or before the Thirty-first Day of *January* in each Year, under a Penalty of Twenty Pounds for each Default ; and the Copy of such Account so sent to the said Clerk of the Peace or Sheriff Clerk shall be kept by him, and shall be open to Inspection by all Persons at all seasonable Hours, on Payment of One Shilling for each Inspection.

Annual Account to be made up by Undertakers, and sent to the Clerk of the Peace in England or Ireland, or to the Sheriff Clerk in Scotland, and to be open to Inspection.

The Gasworks Clauses Act, 1871.
(34 and 35 Vict., c. 41.)

[13th July, 1871.]

Short Title.　2. This Act may be cited as "The Gasworks Clauses Act, 1871."

Accounts, &c.　35. The Undertakers shall fill up and forward to the local authority of every district within the limits of the special Act, on or before the Twenty-fifth day of March in each year, an annual statement of Accounts, made up to the Thirty-first day of December then next preceding, as near as may be in the form and containing the particulars specified in Schedule B. to this Act annexed.

The Undertakers shall keep copies of such annual statement at their office, and sell the same to any applicant at a price not exceeding One Shilling for each such copy.

The Board of Trade, with the consent of the Undertakers, may alter the said forms for the purpose of adapting them to the circumstances of the undertaking, or of better carrying into effect the objects of this Section.

The Waterworks Clauses Act, 1847.
(10 and 11 Vict., c. 17.)

[23rd April, 1847.]

Short Title of this Act.　4. In citing this Act in other Acts of Parliament and in legal Instruments, it shall be enough to use the Expression "The Waterworks Clauses Act, 1847."

And with respect to the Amount of Profit to be received by the Undertakers when the Waterworks are carried on for their benefit, be it enacted as follows :

75. The Profits of the Undertaking to be divided among the Undertakers in any Year shall not exceed the prescribed Rate, or where no rate is prescribed they shall not exceed the Rate of Ten Pounds in the Hundred by the Year on the paid-up Capital in the Undertaking, which in such case shall be deemed the prescribed Rate, unless a larger Dividend be at any Time necessary to make up the Deficiency of any previous Dividend which shall have fallen short of the said yearly Rate. *Profits of the Company to be limited.*

76. If the clear Profits of the Undertaking in any Year amount to a larger Sum than is sufficient, after making up the Deficiency in the Dividends of any previous Year as aforesaid, to make a Dividend at the prescribed Rate, the Excess beyond the Sum necessary for such Purpose shall from Time to Time be invested in Government or other Securities, and the Dividends and Interest arising from such Securities shall also be invested in the same or like Securities, in order that the same may accumulate at Compound Interest until the Fund so formed amounts to the prescribed Sum, or if no sum be prescribed to a Sum equal to One Tenth Part of the nominal Capital of the Un'ertakers, which sum shall form a reserved Fund to answer any Deficiency which may at any Time happen in the Amount of divisible Profits, or to meet any extraordinary Claim or Demand which may at any Time *If Profits exceed the Amount limited Excess to be invested and form a reserved Fund.*

arise against the Undertakers; and if such Fund be at any time reduced it may thereafter be again restored to the said Sum, and so from Time to Time as often as such Reduction shall happen.

Reserved Fund not to be resorted to unless to meet an extraordinary Claim.

77. Provided always, That no Sum of Money shall be taken from the said Fund for the Purpose of meeting any extraordinary Claim, unless it be first certified, in *England* or *Ireland*, by Two Justices, and in *Scotland* by the Sheriff, that the Sum so proposed to be taken is required for the Purpose of meeting any extraordinary Claim within the Meaning of this or the Special Act.

When Fund amounts to prescribed Sum, Interest to be applied to Purposes of the Undertaking.

78. When such Fund shall, by Accumulation or otherwise, amount to the prescribed Sum, or One Tenth Part of the nominal Capital, as the Case may be, the Interest and Dividends thereon shall no longer be invested, but shall be applied to any of the general Purposes of the Undertaking to which the profits thereof are applicable.

If Profits are less than the prescribed Rate, a Sum may be taken from reserved Fund to supply Deficiency.

79. If in any Year the profits of the Undertaking divisible amongst the Undertakers shall not amount to the prescribed Rate, such a Sum may be taken from the reserved Fund as, with the actual divisible Profits of such Year, will enable the Undertakers to make a Dividend of the Amount aforesaid, and so from Time to Time as often as the Occasion shall require.

Annual Account to be made up by Undertakers, and sent to the Clerk of the Peace in England or Ireland, or to

83. And with respect to the yearly Receipt and Expenditure of the Undertakers, be it enacted, That the Undertakers shall, in each Year after they have begun to supply Water under this or the Special Act, cause an Account in abstract to be

prepared of the whole Receipt and Expenditure of all Rates or other Moneys levied under the Powers of this or the Special Act for the Year preceding, under the several distinct Heads of Receipt and Expenditure, with a Statement of the Balance of such Account, duly audited and certified by the Chairman of the Undertakers, and also by the Auditors thereof, if any; and a Copy of such annual Account shall be sent, free of Charge, to the Clerk of the Peace for the County in which the Waterworks are situated, if the Waterworks are situated in *England* or *Ireland*, and if the Waterworks are situated in *Scotland* to the Sheriff Clerk of such County, on or before the Thirty-first Day of *January* in each Year.

[sidenote: the Sheriff Clerk in Scotland, and to be open to Inspection.]

THE METROPOLIS WATER ACT, 1852.
(15 and 16 Vict., c. 84.)

[1st July, 1852.]

19. And with respect to the yearly Receipt and Expenditure of every Company, the Company shall in each Year cause an Account in abstract to be prepared of the whole Receipt and Expenditure of all Rates or other Moneys levied under the Powers of their Act, under the several distinct Heads of Receipt and Expenditure, with a Statement of the Balance of such Account duly audited and certified by the Chairman of the Company, and also by the Auditors thereof, if any, and a Copy of such annual Account shall be sent, free of Charge, to the Town Clerk of the City of *London*, and to the Vestry

[sidenote: Account of Receipt and Expenditure of Rates, &c., to be prepared, and to be open to Inspection.]

Clerk of each Parish supplied with Water by each Company respectively not within the City of *London*, on or before the Thirty-first Day of *January* in each Year.

Short Title.

28. In citing this Act in other Acts and in legal Instruments it shall be enough to use the Expression " The Metropolis Water Act, 1852."

THE METROPOLIS WATER ACT, 1871.
(34 and 35 Vict., c. 113.)

[21st August, 1871.]

Short Title.

1. This Act may be cited for all purposes as " The Metropolis Water Act, 1871.

This and recited Act to be as one.

2. This Act and the Metropolis Water Act, 1852, as the same is amended by this Act, shall be read and construed together as one Act.

Interpretation of Terms.

3. In this Act,—

The expression " the metropolis " shall mean the metropolis as defined by the Metropolis Management Act, 1855 :

The term " Company " shall mean and include any of the companys following : that is to say,—

The Governor and Company of the New River brought from Chadwell and Amwell to London, commonly called " The New River Company ;"

The East London Waterworks ;

The Southwark and Vauxhall Water Company ;

The Company of Proprietors of the West Middlesex Waterworks Company.

The Company of Proprietors of Lambeth Waterworks;

The Governor and Company of Chelsea Waterworks;

The Grand Junction Waterworks Company;

The Company of Proprietors of the Kent Waterworks; and also any other corporation, company, board, commissioners, association, person, persons, or partnership, for the time being supplying water for domestic use within the limits of this Act:

Accounts.

37. Every Company shall, on or before the Thirty first day of July in each year, fill up and forward to the Board of Trade, and to the Town Clerk of the City of London, and to the Metropolitan Board of Works, and to the Vestry Clerk of each parish within which water is supplied by each Company respectively not within the City of London, a statement of account, made up to the end of their financial year then last passed, in such form and containing such particulars as may from time to time be prescribed by the Board of Trade. *Accounts, &c.*

38. There shall be an Auditor of the accounts of the Companies, being a competent and impartial person, from time to time appointed by and removable by the Board of Trade. *Auditor of Accounts.*

There shall be paid to such Auditor such remuneration by the Companies and in such proportions as such Board appoints.

Ascertainment of Capital of Companies.

39. The Auditor shall, with all practicable speed after the passing of this Act, investigate the accounts of the Companies, and ascertain and certify the amounts of their Capitals, distinguishing Share from Loan Capital, and shall ascertain and certify the Capital of each Company, and shall from time to time, as new Capital shall be expended, in like manner ascertain and certify the amount of such new Capital that has been *bonâ fide* expended for the purposes of the undertaking.

Periodical Audit of Accounts.

40. The Auditor shall once in every half year audit the accounts of the Companies.

If he finds the accounts correct he shall certify the same, but if in any instance he finds the accounts of any Company incorrect in principle or in detail, he shall require such Company to correct such accounts in such manner as he thinks right, and no future Dividend shall in any case be declared by any Company until their accounts are certified by the Auditor; provided that the suspension of a Dividend under this Section shall not operate until after the expiration of nine months from the date of the audit.

Facilities for Auditor.

41. Each Company shall, during as well as subsequent to the close of that half year to which the accounts relate, give to the Auditor, his Clerks and Assistants, access to the Books and Documents of such Company, and shall, when required, furnish to him and them all vouchers and information requisite

for the purposes of the audit, and shall afford to him and them all facilities for the proper execution of his and their duty; and any Company making default in complying with any of the provisions of this Section shall, for every such default, be liable to a penalty not exceeding Ten Pounds.

42. If any Company think themselves agrieved by any act or determination of the Auditor, the matter in difference shall be referred to the determination of an Arbitrator agreed on between such Company and the Auditor, or, in default of agreement, appointed, on the application of either party, by the Lord Chief Justice of the Court of Common Pleas; and the reference shall be subject and according to the provisions of the Common Law Procedure Act, 1854; and the decision of the Arbitrator shall be final and conclusive; and, subject to this provision, such Company shall observe and abide by the directions and determinations of the Auditor. *Arbitration between Auditor and Company.*

Penalties.

44. Every penalty incurred by any Company by reason of non-compliance with any of the provisions of this Act shall go and belong to the Metropolitan Authority within the jurisdiction of which the same has been incurred, and may be sued for and recovered by such Metropolitan Authority in any court of competent jurisdiction for the recovery of any ordinary simple contract debt of the like amount, and shall be paid and applied as such Metropolitan Authority shall from time to time direct. *Recovery and Application of Penalties.*

Every such penalty shall be borne and paid (to the satisfaction of the Auditor appointed as in this Act provided) exclusively by and out of the divisible profits of the Company by whom the penalty is incurred, and by way of reduction of Dividend.

THE LIFE ASSURANCE COMPANIES ACT, 1870.
(33 and 34 Vict., c. 61.)

[9th August, 1870.]

Short title.

1. This Act may be cited as " The Life Assurance Companies Act, 1870."

Life Funds separate.

4. In the case of a Company established after the passing of this Act transacting other business besides that of Life Assurance, a separate account shall be kept of all receipts in respect of the Life Assurance and Annuity contracts of the Company, and the said receipts shall be carried to and form a separate fund to be called the Life Assurance Fund of the Company, and such fund shall be as absolutely the security of the life policy and annuity holders as though it belonged to a Company carrying on no other business than that of Life Assurance, and shall not be liable for any contracts of the Company for which it would not have been liable had the business of the Company been only that of Life Assurance ; and in respect to all existing Companies, the exemption of the Life Assurance Fund from liability for other obligations than to its life policy holders shall have reference only to the contracts entered into after the passing of this Act,

unless by the constitution of the Company such exemption already exists : provided always, that this Section shall not apply to any contracts made by any existing Company by the terms of whose Deed of Settlement the whole of the profits of all the business are paid exclusively to the life policy holders, and on the face of which contracts the liability of the assured distinctly appears.

5. From and after the passing of this Act every Company shall, at the expiration of each financial year of such Company, prepare a statement of its revenue account for such year, and of its balance sheet at the close of such year, in the forms respectively contained in the first and second Schedules to this Act. *Statements to be made by Companies.*

6. Every Company which, concurrently with the granting of Policies of Assurance or Annuities on human life, transacts any other kind of Assurance or other business shall, at the expiration of each such financial year as aforesaid, prepare statements of its revenue account for such year, and of its balance sheet at the close of such year, in the forms respectively contained in the third and fourth Schedules of this Act. *Statements by Company doing other than Life Business.*

7. Every Company shall, once in every five years if established after the passing of this Act, and once every ten years if established before the passing of this Act, or at such shorter intervals as may be prescribed by the instrument constituting the Company, or by its regulations or bye-laws, cause an investigation to be made into its financial condition by an Actuary, and shall cause an abstract of the report of *Actuarial Report and Abstract.*

such Actuary to be made in the form prescribed in the fifth Schedule to this Act.

Statement of Life and Annuity Business.

8. Every Company shall, on or before the Thirty-first day of December, One thousand eight hundred and seventy-two, and thereafter within nine months after the date of each such investigation as aforesaid into its financial condition, prepare a statement of its Life Assurance and Annuity business in the form contained in the sixth Schedule to this Act, each of such statements to be made up as at the date of the last investigation, whether such investigation be made previously or subsequently to the passing of this Act: Provided as follows:

> (1.) If the next financial investigation after the passing of this Act of any Company fall during the year One thousand eight hundred and seventy-three, the said statement of such Company shall be prepared within nine months after the date of such investigation, instead of on or before the Thirty-first day of December, One thousand eight hundred and seventy-two.

> (2.) If such investigation be made annually by any Company, such Company may prepare such statement at any time, so that it be made at least once in every three years.

The expression date of each such investigation in this Section shall mean the date to which the accounts of each Company are made up for the purposes of each such investigation.

Forms may be altered.

9. The Board of Trade, upon the applications of or with the consent of a Company, may alter the forms contained in the Schedules to this Act, for the

purpose of adapting them to the circumstances of such Company, or of better carrying into effect the objects of this Act.

10. Every statement or abstract hereinbefore required to be made shall be signed by the Chairman and two Directors of the Company and by the Principal Officer managing the Life Assurance business, and, if the Company has a Managing Director, by such Managing Director, and shall be printed ; and the original, so signed as aforesaid, together with three printed copies thereof, shall be deposited at the Board of Trade within nine months of the dates respectively hereinbefore prescribed as the dates at which the same are to be prepared. And every annual statement so deposited after the next investigation shall be accompanied by a printed copy of the Abstract required to be made by Section seven.

Statements, &c., to be Signed and Printed and Deposited with Board of Trade.

11. A printed copy of the last deposited Statement, Abstract, or other Document by this Act required to be printed shall be forwarded by the Company, by post or otherwise, on application, to every Shareholder and Policy Holder of the Company.

Copies of Statements to be given to Shareholders, &c.

12. Every Company which is not registered under " The Companies Act, 1862," and which has not incorporated in its Deed of Settlement Section Ten of " The Companies Clauses Consolidation Act, 1845," shall keep a " Shareholders Address Book," in accordance with the Provisions of that Section, and shall furnish, on application, to every Shareholder and Policy Holder of the Company a copy of

List of Shareholders.

such book, on payment of a sum not exceeding Sixpence for every hundred words required to be copied for such purpose.

The Friendly Societies Act, 1875.
(38 and 39 Vict., c. 60.)

[11th August, 1875.]

Short title of Act.

1. This Act may be cited as "The Friendly Societies Act, 1875."

Extent of Act.

3. This Act extends to Great Britain and Ireland, the Channel Islands, and the Isle of Man.

As to existing Societies.

6. Every Society now subsisting whose rules have been registered, enrolled, or certified under any Act relating to Friendly Societies or Cattle Insurance Societies, shall be deemed to be a Society registered under this Act, and its rules shall, so far as the same are not contrary to any express provision of this Act, continue in force until altered or rescinded.

Provided that nothing herein contained shall affect the validity of the rules of Friendly Societies established before the Fifteenth day of August, One thousand eight hundred and fifty, notwithstanding that the contingent annual payments to which the members or the nominees of the members of such Societies may become entitled may exceed the limit hereby fixed.

Duties and obligations of Societies.

14. With respect to the duties and obligations of Registered Societies the following provisions shall have effect:

(1.) Every Registered Society shall—

(*c.*) Once at least in every year submit its accounts Audit. for audit either to one of the Public Auditors appointed as herein mentioned, or to two or more persons appointed as the rules of the Society provide, which Auditors shall have access to all the books and accounts of the Society, and shall examine the general statement of the receipts and expenditure, funds and effects of the Society, and verify the same with the accounts and vouchers relating thereto, and shall either sign the same as found by them to be correct, duly vouched, and in accordance with law, or specially report to the Society in what respects they find it incorrect, unvouched, or not in accordance with law :

(*d.*) Once in every year before the first day of Annual June send to the Registrar a general state-Returns. ment (to be called the Annual Return) of the receipts and expenditure, funds and effects of the Society as audited, which shall show separately the expenditure in respect of the several objects of the Society, and shall be made out to the thirty first December then last inclusively, and a copy of the Auditor's Report, if any, shall also be sent to the Registrar with such general statement; and such Annual Return shall state whether the audit has been conducted by a Public Auditor appointed as in this Act provided, and by whom; and, if by any person or persons other than a Public Auditor, shall state the name, address, and calling or profession of each of such persons, and the manner in which and the authority under which they were respectively appointed:

Quinquennial Valuations.

(*f.*) Once at least in the five years next after the commencement of this Act, or the Registry of the Society, and so again within six months after the expiration of every five years succeeding the date of the first valuation under this Act, either cause its assets and liabilities to be valued by a valuer to be appointed by the Society, and send to the Registrar a report, signed by such Valuer, and which shall also state his address and calling or profession, on the condition of the Society, and an abstract to be made by him of the results of his valuation, together with a return containing such information with respect to the benefits assured and contributions receivable by the Society, and of its funds and effects, debts and credits, as the Registrar may from time to time require, or send to the Registrar a return of the benefits assured and contributions receivable from all the members of the Society, and of all its funds and effects, debts and credits, accompanied by such evidence in support thereof as the Chief Registrar prescribes,

in which case the Registrar shall cause
the assets and liabilities of the Society to
be valued and reported on by some Actuary,
and shall send to the Society a copy of his
report, and an abstract of the results of his
valuation :

(*i.*) Keep a copy of the last annual balance sheet
for the time being, and of the last quinquennial valuation for the time being,
together with the report of the Auditors,
if any, always hung up in a conspicuous
place at the registered office of the Society.

(5.) Every annual, quinquennial, or other return, Returns to be
abstract of valuation, and other document required in prescribed
Form.
for the purposes of this Act shall be made in such
form and shall contain such particulars as the Chief
Registrar prescribes.

Provided that the Chief Registrar, with the ap- In what Case
proval of the Treasury, may dispense with the quin- Quinquennial Returns, &c.,
quennial return and with the valuation herein may be dis-
pensed with.
required in respect of Societies to whose purposes
or to the nature of whose operations he may deem
the same inapplicable ; and may also dispense with
the quinqennial return in cases where, at the request
of a Society, he may, by inspection of the books
thereof through any person whom he appoints,
obtain such information as he deems sufficient of
the sickness and mortality experienced by the
Society ; and the provisions herein contained in
respect of the quinquennial return and valuation
shall not apply to Benevolent Societies, Working
Men's Clubs, or Cattle Insurance Societies, nor to

specially authorised Societies, unless it be so directed in the authority for registering the same.

Property and Funds of Societies. 16. With respect to the property and funds of registered Societies, the following provisions shall have effect:

Investment of Funds. (1.) The Trustees, with the consent of the Committee of Management or of a majority of the members of a Society present and entitled to vote in general meeting, may from time to time invest the funds of such Society, or any part thereof, to any amount in any of the following ways:

(a.) In the Post Office Savings Bank, or in any Savings Bank certified under the Act of 1863:

(b.) In the Public Funds:

(c.) With the Commissioners for the Reduction of the National Debt as hereinafter provided:

(d.) In the purchase of land, or in the erection or alteration of offices or other buildings thereon.

(e.) Upon any other security expressly directed by the rules of the Society, not being personal security, except as hereinafter authorised with respect to Loans.

Holding of Land. (2.) A Society, or any branch of a Society, may (if the rules thereof so provide) hold, purchase, or take on lease in the names of the Trustees for the time being of such Society or branch, in every county where it has an office, any land, and may sell, exchange, mortgage, lease, or build upon the same (with power to alter and pull down buildings and again rebuild), and no purchaser, assignee, mortgagee, or tenant shall be bound to inquire as to the authority for any sale, exchange, mortgage, or lease by the trustees, and the receipt of the trustees shall be a discharge for all moneys arising from or in connection with such sale, exchange, mortgage, or lease ; and for the purpose of this Section no branch of a registered Society need be separately registered. Provided that nothing herein contained shall authorise any Benevolent Society to hold land exceeding one acre in extent at any one time.

(3.) All property belonging to a Society, whether acquired before or after the same is registered, shall vest in the Trustees for the time being of the Society, for the use and benefit of the Society and the members thereof, and of all persons claiming through the members according the rules of the Society; and the property of any branch of a Society shall vest in the Trustees of such branch, or in the Trustess of the Society if the rules of the Society so provide, for the use and benefit either of the members of such branch and persons claiming through such members, or of the members of the Society generally, and persons claiming through them, according to the rules of the Society. *Property of Society, how vested.*

18. With respect to Loans to members of registered Societies, the following provisions shall have effect : *Loans to Members.*

(1.) Not more than one half of the amount of an assurance on the life of a member of at least one full year's standing may be advanced to him, on the written security of himself and two satisfactory sureties for repayment ; and the amount advanced, with all interest thereon, may be deducted from the sum assured, without prejudice in the meantime to the operation of such security.

Loans may be made out of separate Loan Fund. (2.) A Society may, out of any separate Loan Fund to be formed by contributions or deposits of its members, make Loans to its members on their personal security, with or without sureties, as may be provided by the rules, subject to the following restrictions :

> (*a.*) No Loan can at any time be made out of moneys contributed for the other purposes of the Society.
>
> (*b.*) No member shall be capable of holding any interest in the Loan Fund exceeding Two Hundred Pounds :
>
> (*c.*) No Society shall make any Loan to a member on personal security beyond the amount fixed by the rules, or shall make any Loan which, together with any moneys for the time being owing by a member to the Society, shall exceed Fifty Pounds :
>
> (*d.*) No Society shall hold at any one time on deposit from its members any moneys beyond the amount fixed by the rules, which shall not exceed two thirds of the total sums for the time being owing to the Society by the members who have borrowed from the Loan Fund.

Societies receiving Contributions by Collectors. 30. The provisions of the present Section apply only to Friendly Societies and, except as after mentioned, Industrial Assurance Companies receiving contributions by means of Collectors at a greater distance than ten miles from the registered office of the Society.

(6.) At least one General Meeting of the Society shall be held in every year. *One General Meeting every Year.*

(8.) A copy of every Balance Sheet of a Society shall, during the seven days next preceding the meeting at which the same is to be presented, be kept open by the Society for inspection at every office at which the business of the Society is carried on, and shall be delivered or sent prepaid to every member on demand. *Balance Sheets.*

(9.) The Annual Returns shall be certified by some person not an officer of the Society (otherwise than as Auditor thereof), carrying on publicly the business of an accountant, and if not so certified shall be deemed not to have been made. *Certification of Annual Returns.*

32. With respect to penalties under this Act, the following provisions shall have effect : *Penalties.*

(1.) If any person wilfully makes, orders, or allows to be made, any entry, erasure in, or omission from any Balance Sheet of a registered Society, or any Contribution or Collecting Book, or any return or document required to be sent, produced, or delivered for the purposes of this Act, with intent to falsify the same, or to evade any of the provisions of this Act, he is liable to a penalty not exceeding Fifty Pounds. *Penalty for Falsification.*

35. The Treasury may from time to time appoint Public Auditors and Valuers for the purposes of this Act, and may determine from time to time the rates of renumeration to be paid by Societies for the services of such Auditors and Valuers ; but *Public Auditors.*

the employment of such Auditors and Valuers is not compulsory on any Society.

THE FRIENDLY SOCIETIES AMENDMENT ACT, 1876.
(39 & 40 Vict., c. 32.)

[24th July, 1876.]

Construction of Act.

Short title.

1. This Act shall be construed as one with the Friendly Societies Act, 1875 (herein termed "the Principal Act,") and may be cited as "The Friendly Societies Amendment Act, 1876," or together with the Principal Act as "The Friendly Societies Acts."

Registered Societies may contribute to Funds of other Societies.

4. Nothing in the Principal Act or in this Act contained shall prevent any registered Society or branch from contributing to the Funds or taking part by delegates or otherwise in the government of any other registered Society or registered branch of a Society, as may be provided in the rules of such first-named Society or branch, without becoming a branch under the Friendly Societies Acts of such other Society or branch.

THE INDUSTRIAL AND PROVIDENT SOCIETIES ACT, 1876.
(39 & 40 Vict., c. 45.)

[11th August, 1876.]

Short title of Act.

1. This Act may be cited as the Industrial and Provident Societies Act, 1876.

Extent of Act.

2. This Act shall extend to Great Britain and Ireland, and the Channel Islands.

5. Every incorporated Society now subsisting Existing Societies. whose rules have been registered or certified under any Act relating to Industrial and Provident Societies, shall be deemed to be a Society registered under this Act, and its rules shall, so far as the same are not contrary to any express provision of this Act, continue in force until altered or rescinded.

10. With respect to the duties and obligations of Duties and Obligations of registered Societies the following provisions shall Societies. have effect :

(1.) Every Society shall—

(c.) Once at least in every year submit its accounts Audit. for audit either to one of the Public Auditors appointed as herein mentioned, or to two or more persons appointed, as the rules of the Society provide, who shall have access to all the books and accounts of the Society, and shall examine the general statements of the receipts and expenditure, funds and effects of the Society, and verify the same with the accounts and vouchers relating thereto, and shall either sign the same as found by them to be correct, duly vouched, and in accordance with law, or specially report to the Society in what respects they find it incorrect, unvouched, or not in accordance with law.

(d.) Once in every year before the first day of Annual Returns. June send to the Registrar a general statement (to be called the Annual Return) of the receipts and expenditure, funds, and effects of the Society as audited, which shall show separately the expenditure in respect of the several objects of the Society, and shall be made out to the thirty-first December then last inclusively, and shall state whether the audit has been conducted by a Public Auditor appointed as by this Act is provided, and by whom, and if by any person other than a Public Auditor, shall state the name, address, and calling or profession of each such person, and the manner in which and the authority under which he is appointed, and together therewith shall send a copy of the Auditor's Report :

Balance Sheet, &c., to be hung up at Office.

(*g.*) Keep a copy of the last Balance Sheet for the time being, together with the Report of the Auditors, always hung up in a conspicuous place at the registered office of the Society.

Provisions as to Banking.

(2.) The following provisions shall apply to the business of Banking by Societies—

(*a.*) No Society which has any withdrawable share capital shall carry on the business of Banking :

(*b.*) Every Society which carries on the business of Banking shall, on the first Mondays in February and August in each year, make out and keep conspicuously hung up in its registered office, and every other place of business belonging to it, a statement in the form in the third Schedule hereto annexed, or as near thereto as the circumstances admit.

12. With respect to the property and funds of Property and Funds of registered Societies, the following provisions shall Societies. have effect :

(1.) A Society may (if its rules do not direct Holding of Land. otherwise) hold, purchase, or take on lease in its own name any land, and may sell, exchange, mortgage, lease, or build upon the same (with power to alter and pull down buildings and again rebuild).

(4.) A Society may, if its rules so allow, invest Investments. any part of its capital in the shares or on the security of any other Society registered under this Act or under the Building Societies Acts, or of any Company registered under the Companies Acts or incorporated by Act of Parliament or by Charter, provided that no such investment be made in the shares of any Society or Company other than one with Limited Liability, and a Society so investing may make such investment in its registered name and shall be deemed to be a person within the meaning of the Companies Acts, 1862 and 1867, and the Building Societies Act, 1874, and any investment made before the passing of this Act which would have been valid if this Act had been then in force is hereby made valid and confirmed.

(5.) Any other Body Corporate may, if its regula- Other Corporate Bodies. tions permit, hold shares by its corporate name in a Society.

(7.) The Profits of the Society may be applied to Application of profits. any lawful purpose.

Penalties.

18. With respect to Penalties under this Act, the following provisions shall have effect:

Penalty for Falsification.

(1.) If any person wilfully makes, orders, or allows to be made any entry or erasure in, or omission from any Balance Sheet of a registered Society, or any contribution or collecting book, or any return or document required to be sent, produced, or delivered for the purposes of this Act, with intent to falsify the same, or to evade any of the provisions of this Act, he shall be liable to a penalty not exceeding Fifty Pounds.

Public Auditors.

21. The Treasury may from time to time apoint Public Auditors for the purposes of this Act, and may determine from time to time the rates of remuneration to be paid by Societies for the services of such Auditors; but the employment of such Auditors is not compulsory on any Society.

THE FALSIFICATION OF ACCOUNTS ACT, 1875.
(38 and 39 Vict., c. 24.)

[29th June, 1875.]

Punishment for Falsification of Accounts, &c.

1. If any Clerk, Officer, or Servant, or any person employed or acting in the capacity of a Clerk, Officer, or Servant, shall wilfully and with intent to defraud destroy, alter, mutilate, or falsify any book, paper, writing, valuable security, or account which belong to or is in the possession of his employer, or has been received by him for or on behalf of his employer, or shall wilfully and with intent to defraud make or concur in making any false entry in, or omit or alter, or concur in omitting or altering, any material particular from or in any such book, or any document or account, then in every such case the person so offending shall be guilty of a misdemeanour, and be liable to be kept in penal servitude for a term not exceeding seven years, or to be imprisoned with or without hard labour for any term not exceeding two years.

2. It shall be sufficient in any indictment under this Act to allege a general intent to defraud, without naming any particular person intended to be defrauded. *Intention to Defraud sufficient Indictment.*

3. This Act shall be read as one with the Act of the twenty-fourth and twenty-fifth of Her Majesty, chapter ninety-six. *Act to be read with 24 & 25 Vict. c. 96.*

4. This Act may be cited as the Falsification of Accounts Act, 1875. *Short title.*

CHAPTER IV.

PRINCIPLES OF BOOK-KEEPING IN USE BY JOINT STOCK COMPANIES.

Auditor should understand Bookkeeping—Registry or Statistical Books—Application for, and Allotment of, Shares Book— Register of Members—Register of Shareholders—Shareholders' Address Book—Register of Holders of Consolidated Stock—Register of Mortgages—Register of Transfers— Register of Debenture Stock—Register of Directors and Managers—Annual List of Members—Minute Books— Financial or Account Books—Cash Book— Petty Cash Book—Day Book—Invoice Book—Bills Receivable Book— Bills Payable Book—Journal—Ledger—Trial Balance— Difference between Trial Balance and Balance Sheet.

Auditor should understand Bookkeeping,

ONE of the most important qualifications an Auditor should possess is a thorough knowledge of, and experience in, Commercial Book-keeping, but as (very often unfortunately for themselves) a meeting of Shareholders does not always in its selection of an Auditor take this into consideration, it is necessary that a short description be given of the Books of Account ordinarily made use of in the offices of public Companies.

There are so many works on Book-keeping already published, that it is not necessary to enter into an explanation of the system generally, but as no treatise intended to embrace the various details which come under the observation of an Auditor in the prosecution of his Audit would be complete without reference to so important a part of his duties, a short description of the Books in general use by Public Companies is given.

Some of these Books need not be referred to by the Auditor at every Audit, but should he at any time not be satisfied with the Accounts and Documents placed before him he may deem it necessary to examine some, or even all of them, for the purpose of his investigation. *Certain Books need not be examined by the Auditor at every Audit.*

The books used by Public Companies are as numerous as the ingenuity of Managers, Accountants, and Secretaries have been able to devise, and as very frequently the official to whom is entrusted the important duty of modelling and opening them has been previously engaged in a different class of business, it often happens that unnecessary columns, accompanied by equally unnecessary detail, are introduced into the books.

An efficient Auditor would, if necessary, be able to remedy this and to suggest more suitable forms for adoption, but it would be impossible in this work to prescribe the forms of books for recording the transactions in detail of every class of Company.

The second part of the present chapter is devoted to an explanation of the general system of Book-keeping suitable for Companies, by means of which these details are properly recorded.

The Books in use by Public Companies may be divided into two classes : *Books in use by Public Companies.*

1. Registry or Statistical.
2. Financial or Account.

Registry or Statistical Books.

Registry or Statistical Books.

The attention of the Auditor is principally confined to the Financial Books, and it does not ordinarily come within his province to investigate the Statistical ones or Books of Record, every Company having few or many according to the nature of its business. The following, however, should certainly be inspected or referred to by him, some of which are prescribed by Act of Parliament, the others by general practice and custom.

Application for and allotment of Shares Book.

Register of Members (25 and 26 Vict., cap. 89, sec. 25).

Register of Shareholders (8 Vict., cap. 16, sec. 9).

Shareholders' Address Book (8 Vict., cap. 16, sec. 10 ; 33 and 34 Vict., cap. 61, sec. 12.)

Register of Holders of Consolidated Stock (8 Vict., cap. 16, sec. 63).

Register of Mortgages (8 Vict., cap. 16, sec. 45; 25 and 26 Vict., cap. 89, sec. 43).

Register of Transfers.

Register of Debenture Stock (26 and 27 Vict., cap. 118, sec. 28).

Register of Directors and Managers (25 and 26 Vict., cap. 89, sec. 45).

Annual List of Members and Summary Book (25 and 26 Vict., cap, 81, sec. 26).

Minute Book (8 Vict., cap. 16, sec. 98 ; 25 and 26 Vict., cap. 89, sec. 67).

Members' Minute Book.

Application for, and Allotment of, Shares Book.

The application for and allotment of Shares Book should contain the names, addresses, and occupations of all applicants for Shares entered in the order in which their applications are received at the office of the Company, together with the number of Shares they each apply for, the number of Shares allotted to them in respect of such application, the dates of application, of receipt of application, and of allotment, the numerical number of the Shares allotted, the date of the issue of the Certificates, and any other particulars the Directors or Manager may consider it desirable to have recorded.

A Register of Members is required to be kept by every Company registered under the Companies Act, 1862. This must contain the names, addresses, and occupations of the Members, a statement of the Shares held by each Member, distinguishing each Share by its number, the amount paid, or agreed to be considered as paid, on the Shares of each Member, also the dates on which their names are entered on the Register, and the dates on which they cease to be Members of the Company. *Register of Members.*

Frequently the Shareholders' Ledger is so designed as to contain all these particulars and thus two Books are amalgamated in one. This plan has, however, one great disadvantage. Section 32 of the Companies Act, 1862, prescribes that the Register of Members shall be open to the inspection of any Member gratis, and to that of any other person on the payment of one shilling, or any less sum the Company may prescribe for each inspection. It might be very undesirable for the Company to throw open its Share Ledger to the inspection of any one making a demand under this Section, and for this *Frequently Amalgamated with Shareholders' Ledger.*

reason the Shareholders' Ledger is usually kept as a separate Book. The Book which gives all the particulars required by the Act, without affording any information to an inspector except by considerable research, is one which contains the Shares in numerical order, with the names of their respective holders, and other particulars, in the same line with the number.

By Section 30 of the Act, just referred to, no notice of any trust expressed, implied, or constructive, shall be entered in the Register of Members.

Register of Shareholders. Companies incorporated by Special Act of Parliament are required by the Companies Clauses Consolidation Act, 1845, to keep a Book, called a " Register of Shareholders," in which the names, arranged in alphabetical order, of the individuals and corporations holding Shares in the Company are entered, together with the number of Shares they hold, distinguishing each Share by its number and the amount paid on such Shares. At each Ordinary Meeting of the Shareholders the Common Seal of the Company is affixed to this Register for the purpose of authentication.

Shareholders' Address Book. These Companies, and also all Life Assurance Companies not registered under the Companies Act, 1862, and which have not incorporated in their Deeds of Settlement Section 10 of the Companies Clauses Consolidation Act, 1845, are obliged to keep a " Shareholders' Address Book," in which are entered in alphabetical order the names and addresses of the Shareholders.

Register of Holders of Consolidated Stock. A Register of Holders of Consolidated Stock has also to be kept by Companies incorporated by Special

Acts of Parliament, and should contain the names of the proprietors of the Stock and the amounts they hold respectively.

Limited Companies registered under the Companies Act, 1862, and also Companies incorporated by Special Act of Parliament, are obliged to keep a Register of Mortgages and charges given by them which specifically affect the property of the Company. *Register of Mortgages.*

This Register should contain a short description of the property mortgaged or charged, each mortgage or charge being separately entered, also the names of the Mortgagees or persons entitled to such charges with the amounts of charge created.

Nearly all Companies keep a Register of Tranfers (and Companies incorporated by Special Act of Parliament are obliged to do so), in which is entered the names and addresses of the transferors and transferees of any Shares or Stock, also the particulars and amount of the Shares, or the amount of the Stock transferred. *Register of Transfers.*

Companies incorporated by special Act have also to keep a " Register of Debenture Stock," in which is entered the names and addresses of the several persons and corporations holding the Debenture Stock, with the amounts of the Stock to which they are respectively entitled. *Register of Debenture Stock.*

Mutual Companies, registered under the Companies Act, 1862, have to keep at their registered office a Register containing the names, addresses, and the occupations of its Directors and Managers. *Mutual Companies to keep a Register of Directors and Managers.*

A copy of this Register has to be sent to the Registrar of Joint Stock Companies, and any change that takes place therein has to be at once notified to him.

Annual List of Members. Section 26 of the Companies Act, 1862, prescribes that every Company registered under that Act, having a capital divided into shares, shall keep an Annual List of Members, together with a summary. The particulars which have to be entered in this book will be found in the Appendix.

Minute Book. The Minute Book should contain a record of the Directors present at each Board meeting, and of all their transactions thereat.

As the Auditor may frequently have to refer to this Book, he should see that it is properly kept. All agreements entered into by the Directors should be placed on record in this Book, also the cheques drawn, discussions of importance and their result, and, in fact, all that transpires at meetings of the Board, with the exception of mere conversation.

Committee Minute Books. In large Companies the Directors divide their routine business among Committees of their body, each of which has its own Minute Book. The above remarks, however, apply whether the Minutes are recorded in one or more Books.

Shareholders' Minute Book. A Minute Book should also be kept of the transactions of the meetings of the Shareholders, to which the Auditor should refer for resolutions affecting the accounts.

Financial or Account Books.

The following Account Books are generally used by public Companies, in non-trading Companies the Day Book and Invoice Book are known by other names.

Cash Book.

Petty Cash Book.

Day Book.

Invoice Book.

Bills Receivable Book.

Bills Payable Book.

Journal.

Ledger.

The Cash Book, as its name implies, contains a record of the receipts and expenditure of the Company. It should, however except in the case of very small Companies, only contain those payments which are either made by cheques, or bills payable, and bank charges. All payments for which cheques are not drawn should be entered in a subsidiary book, called the " Petty Cash Book," to provide for which payment cheques for round sums should be drawn, and entered in the Cash Book to the debit of petty cash, to be accounted for in the subsidiary book.

The Cash Book is therefore practically a counterpart of the Bankers' Pass Book, and they can easily be checked together.

All monetary receipts, coin, bank notes, cheques, bankers' drafts and orders are, of course, entered in the Cash Book, including the capital as received, premiums on shares, also the cheques drawn by the Company on its bankers, bank charges, and bank interest. When Bills of Exchange Receivable are discounted the proceeds are, of course, brought into the receipt side of the Cash Book, while on the other side should be entered the amount charged by the bankers for the accommodation.

Petty Cash Book. The Petty Cash Book contains, as already mentioned, a record of those payment for which it would be inconvenient, or the amounts of which would be considered too small, to draw for each a separate cheque.

Instead of posting each of the items in the Petty Cash Book to the debit of their Ledger Accounts, an abstract may be made monthly, journalised, and then posted into the Ledger.

Day Book. The Day Book contains the records of all goods sold and delivered by a trading Company, these should be entered in detail, and the amount charged for each item placed in a cash column.

The totals of the cash columns are carried in the usual way through the Journal to the credit of a general sales or a departmental account, while each sale is usually posted direct into the Ledger to the debit of the purchaser of the goods.

When a business is divided into several departments each department has usually its own Day Book.

Equivalent for Day Book in Non-trading Companies. In non-trading Companies books of record of the business transacted are kept on very much the same principle as the Day Book of a trading Company, their object being to ensure that the Accounts of the customers in the Ledger are debited with the

proper amounts, also that these amounts are carried
either in detail, or in total, periodically to the credit
of an impersonal Account in the Ledger, from which
they will be ultimately transferred to the credit of
the Revenue, or Profit and Loss Account.

In the Invoice or Bought Book are entered, with *Invoice Book.*
full particulars, the purchases, by a trading Company, of all goods intended to be sold again.

The Invoices themselves should be numbered and
filed, in numerical order. For the purpose of facili-
tating reference, the numbers should coincide with
those in the Invoice Book.

Bills are written undertakings to pay certain sums *Bills of Exchange.*
on certain dates, and can be drawn in two forms, as
acceptances, or as promissory notes, the former
being more generally used in commercial transactions.

The Bills Receivable Book contains the particulars *Bills Receivable and Bills Payable Book.*
of those Bills, the proceeds of which, on maturity,
are paid to the Company, while the particulars of
those Bills, which have to be paid by the Company
on their due date, are entered in the Bills Payable
Book.

When a customer gives a Bill Receivable to the
Company in lieu of cash his Ledger Account is at
once credited with the amount of the Bill, while the
Bills Receivable Account in the Ledger is debited
with a like amount. In the same way when the
Company discharges one of its obligations by giving
a Bill Payable the firm receiving the Bill is debited
with the amount, and the Bills Payable Account in
the Ledger is at the same time credited.

Journal   The Journal is the Book which constitutes the
system of book-keeping by double entry. Into it
are collected, either in detail or in abstract form,
the transactions of the Company previously entered
in the Books already described, or in those corresponding to them.

Particulars to   The Journal has two cash columns, usually on
be entered
therein.   the same page, with an additional column for the
Ledger folios. In the left, or debit cash column, are
entered the amounts which have to be posted to the
debit of Accounts in the Ledger, while in the right
hand cash column are entered those amounts which
have to be posted to the credit of Ledger accounts.

As a check on the correctness of the figures, the
columns should be added up on the completion of
the entries for the time being, and if the totals of
the two columns agree the items can be posted into
the Ledger.

Opening   The first entries in the Journal of a Company
entries in
Journal of a   formed for acquiring a property, or taking over a
new
Company.   business, would be those referring to the purchase,
the entries being made for the purpose of bringing
into the accounts any property or other asset, the
particulars of which would be contained in the
deed, also any charges, if any, with which the
property is encumbered.

All sales, purchases, interest, discount, commission, expenses, &c., should be journalised, also the
Bills Payable and Receivable. In fact, to fully carry
out the system of book-keeping by double entry,
every item in the subsidiary books should be journalised, and posted from the Journal into the Ledger.

It is, however, usual to post the Day Book and Invoice Book entries direct to the debit or credit of the personal Accounts in the Ledger, also the cash receipts and payments. In some Companies the cash is partly journalised as regards certain entries, the remainder being posted direct.

The Ledger contains the classification of all the Ledger. entries in the other financial books, and no other entries, with the exception of transfers from one Ledger account to another, should be made in it, as in strict accordance with the theory of double entry, as practised in this country, all items found in the Ledger should have passed through the Journal, and been posted into the Ledger therefrom.

In order, however, to avoid needless repetition, it is the practice, as already stated, to post the items in the Cash Book direct into the Ledger, also the debits and credits of the personal Accounts from the Day Book and Invoice Books, or their equivalents. These are, however, the only exception.

Before preparing the Revenue Account and Trial Balance Sheet, the balances of the Ledger Accounts, Balance. both personal and impersonal, should be taken out and a summary made of them, the debit and credit balances being in two separate columns.

This is called a " Trial Balance," and when the totals of the two columns coincide (including the Cash Book balance) it is correct, and is a proof of the accuracy of the postings. From the " Trial Balance " the Revenue Account and Balance Sheet are prepared.

In many companies the duties of the Book-keeper

terminate with the preparation of the "Trial Balance," the manipulation of this document, represented by the drawing up of the Revenue Account and Balance Sheet, being frequently entrusted to the Auditor, when that official is a Chartered Accountant.

Difference
between the
Trial Balance
and the
Balance
Sheet.

The Trial Balance must not be confounded with the Balance Sheet, the former contains merely the balances of the Ledger Accounts, the total of the debit balances, of which must agree with that of the credit balances. The Balance Sheet consists of the debit and credit balances of the Ledger after the Revenue or Profit and Loss Account has been closed, and the profit or loss, as the case may be, has been ascertained, that is, it shows on one side the actual liabilities of the Company, while on the other are enumerated the assets.

The preceding remarks explain the system of Book-keeping in general use by public Companies. With reference to the subsidiary Books, it would, as stated at the commencement of the chapter, be impossible to prescribe the forms for every class of Company.

The Books necessarily vary according to the nature of the business, but the object for which they are employed is always the same, namely, to record the transactions in as simple a manner as is consistent to ensure perfect accuracy, combined with rapidity in the transfer.

CHAPTER V.

NATURE AND PRINCIPLES OF AN AUDIT.

Nature of an effective Audit—Errors of Omission—Errors of Commission—Errors of Principle—A List of the Books of Assistance to the Auditor—Auditor should be provided with the Regulations—Investigation of the Capital Account —Prospectus—Application for Shares—Letters of Allotment—Share Certificates—Entries in the Books of the Particulars of the Purchase—Examination of the Cash Book—Of the Vouchers—Documents should be arranged for the Inspection of the Auditor—Reconciliation of the Balances of the Cash Book and Bankers' Pass Book—Examination of the subsidiary Books.

WHEN the Accounts of a Public Company are ready for the Auditor it is usual for the Secretary of such Company to communicate with the Auditor to that effect, who thereupon fixes a time when he will attend at the Office of the Company for the purpose of commencing his investigation. *Intimation should be sent to the Auditor when Accounts are ready for him.*

Before giving a detailed description of the duties it is usually incumbent upon an Auditor to fulfil, it is desirable to state shortly the nature of an Audit in order to correct a notion which prevails that this is represented by checking the Ledger balances into the Balance Sheet, the additions in the Cash Book, *Nature of an Audit.*

the postings therefrom and the other books into the Ledger, and comparing the payments made with the vouchers produced.

An Audit to be effectual, that is, to enable the Auditor to certify as to the accuracy of the Accounts presented, may for practical purposes be divided into three parts, namely, to guard against (1) Errors of Omission; (2) Errors of Commission; and (3) Errors of Principle.

Errors of Omission. With regard to " Errors of Omission," each item which appears either on the debit side of the Balance Sheet or the Cash Book should be checked as far as possible by an original document obtained from an independent source, in order to ascertain that the Company has charged itself with all cash received or liability incurred.

For example, in the case of the first audit of a Company's Accounts it is necessary to check the letters of application and allotment against the amounts shown in the Cash Book as having been received on Capital account, and in regard to the liabilities in respect of purchases, the postings in the Ledger should be checked through the subsidiary books, so as to ascertain that the balances are all brought to the debit side of the Balance Sheet.

Errors of Commission. Respecting " Errors of Commission," it is a comparatively simple task to detect any errors of this nature that may exist, as it is a mere mechanical process to check the items of one book with the corresponding items of another until they are brought into the Ledger, and from thence finally carried into the Revenue Account or Balance Sheet, or to compare the amounts taken credit for as payments with the vouchers produced.

With regard to " Errors of Principle," when the Auditor is a Chartered Accountant the details of the Audit, such as checking the items from one book into another, examining the vouchers, &c., are usually entrusted to clerks working under his superintendence, the Auditor reserving for himself the duty of ascertaining if any Errors of Principle have been committed, such as, That the authorised Capital of the Company, both Share and Loan, has not been exceeded. That Expenditure, which ought properly to be charged against the Revenue Account, has not been capitalised. That the Funds of the Company have not been invested in prohibited securities, &c. *Errors of Principle.*

The Auditor, before entering upon the duties of his first audit of a Company's Accounts may find it very useful to have in his possession a complete List of the Books in use by the Company, both financial and statistical. *A List of the Books of great service to the Auditor.*

A careful perusal of this list will, in conjunction with any verbal explanation he may think it advisable to obtain from the officials, make the Auditor acquainted with the nature of the business, and also with the system on which it is conducted and its transactions recorded, which knowledge an Auditor will consider most essential he should obtain before commencing his examination of the books.

The Secretary should also be requested to supply him with a copy of the original prospectus if the *Auditor should be Provided*

Company be a new one, also a copy of the Memorandum and Articles of Association should the Company have been registered under the Companies Act, 1862, a copy of the Act if the Company has been incorporated by special Act or Acts of Parliament, or a copy of the rules in the case of a Society registered under the Friendly Societies or Industrial and Provident Societies Acts.

This should be carefully perused, and special notice should be taken of those Sections which in any way relate to or have any bearing on the Accounts of the Company or Society, or the duties of the Auditors.

Should these not be referred to, the Auditor will of course, be guided by the Public Acts under which the Company or Society is registered, the Sections of which demanding his attention will be found in Chapter III.

When special instructions are given in the Articles of Association or in the Private Acts or Rules as to how the Accounts are to be presented to the Shareholders, and how they are to be certified by the Auditors, the Sections containing these instructions are the Regulations to which he is to conform. If they only give partial directions they are to be read in conjunction with the Public Acts.

Investigation
of the Capital
Account. At the first audit of the Accounts of a Company the Share Capital should be investigated, and the Auditor should ascertain that the Share and Loan Capital is not in excess of the amounts authorised by the Articles of Association or the private Acts by which the Company has been incorporated.

The contract existing between a Company and its Prospectus.
individual Shareholders is almost invariably represented by a Prospectus, which is accompanied by a
form of Application for Shares The latter usually Application
consists of two parts, one being the actual applica- for Shares.
tion for the number of Shares the applicant wishes
to acquire in the Company. This is signed by him
and addressed to the Directors, informing them that
he has paid to the Bankers of the Company the application money on these Shares, and requesting them
to allot him these Shares, also agreeing to become
a member of the Company in respect of such Shares
in accordance with the terms of the Prospectus, or
in respect of any less number the Directors may
allot in respect of such application, and authorising
his name to be placed on the Register of Members
for the Shares so allotted.

The other part of the form of application is the
Bankers' receipt, which is forwarded by the applicant
for Shares to the Bankers of the Company, together
with the amount which the Prospectus states must
be paid on application for Shares, in order to treat
the application as a *bonâ-fide* one, and one on which
the Directors would feel justified in making an allotment.

The Bankers' receipt is signed by the Bankers,
returned to the applicant, and is retained by him.
The applications for Shares are placed before the
Board, and Letters of Allotment are forwarded to Letters of
those whose applications are accepted. When the Allotment.
total number of Shares applied for do not exceed the
number proposed to be issued, the full number are

usually allotted to the applicants, but when they exceed the proposed issue the Directors usually allot *pro rata.*

Share Certificates. When the Share Certificates have been prepared they are forwarded to the Shareholders in exchange for the Letters of Allotment. These, together with the applications for Shares, should be filed in the Offices of the Company. By these means the contract between the Shareholder and the Company is made complete, and the evidence on which the contract is based is duly recorded.

Frequently, in small Companies, the Prospectus directs that the payments on application are to be sent to the office. The Auditor should then be particularly careful to ascertain that they have been properly accounted for.

Entries in the Books of Account of Particulars of the Purchase Money. The Auditor should also see that proper entries have been made in the Books of Account for recording the particulars of the purchase of any property or business, to acquire which the Company was formed, also any charges there may have been on the property at the time of its passing into the possession of the Company. **Also of Mortgages.** He should also ascertain that all Mortgages, or Bonds issued of the nature of a Mortgage are duly recorded and registered in accordance with the Acts.

Examination of the Cash Book. Having satisfied himself as regards the Share Capital, the Auditor may then devote his attention to the Cash Book.

The debit or income side should be checked with the most independent source the Auditor can find available—for example, the counterfoils of receipt books, the counter cash book of an Insurance Company, or the customers' pass books of a Bank.

The items on the credit side of the Cash Book should be checked with the Vouchers for the payments. This is, of course, a mere mechanical process, but unfortunately among the unprofessional, that is, the majority of Auditors, is considered the only part of their duties really demanding any care or attention. *Of the Vouchers.*

The perusal of this treatise will, however, it is hoped, correct this impression, and show that an effectual audit of the accounts of a public Company involves a far greater amount of experience, skill, and labour, than is required for the mere checking and vouching the expenditure of the cash, and ascertaining that the accounts, as presented to the Shareholders, agrees with the books kept by the Company.

The Auditor has a right to demand that the Vouchers should be either kept in a Guard Book or filed in some other way, in the order of the corresponding entries in the Cash Book, so as to facilitate ready reference, and to prevent his time being unreasonably taken up by his having to search for each Voucher. *Vouchers should be filed.*

It may be here remarked that the Auditor will find it greatly facilitate his work if he makes it a rule not to accept any papers handed to him for his inspection which are not properly arranged. *All Documents required by the Auditors should be arranged.*

It very frequently happens, especially in the offices of small Companies, that on the Auditor asking for the Vouchers for the cash payments, he is handed a bundle of receipted accounts, and on attempting to

7

check them with the Cash Book he ascertains many are missing. Much time is, in consequence, lost in looking for these, or in obtaining duplicates, while, if the Vouchers were previously arranged, missing ones would be found or fresh ones obtained.

Vouchers should consist of actual Receipts. The Vouchers should principally, if not entirely, consist of actual Receipts, and, in checking the payments to merchants or tradesmen, with the exception of those made by Bills Payable, the Auditor should require the Receipts to be produced. In certain instances, however, the endorsements on the cheques may be accepted as sufficient proof that the money has been expended in the manner stated.

Reconciliation of the Balance of the Cash Book and of the Bankers' Pass Book. The Balance, as shown in the Cash Book, should be checked with the Balance in the Bankers' Pass Book. These are very seldom identical, as cheques drawn by the Company may not have been presented for payment on or before the day on which the books are closed, neither will the bankers, unless a special arrangement has been made with them, have given credit for country cheques not cleared on that day.

In order to facilitate checking these balances, a Reconciliation Statement, which may be entered in the Cash Book, should be prepared for the Auditor. This should commence with the balance as shown in the Cash Book, to which should he added the amounts of the cheques outstanding. From the total thus obtained should be deducted the amount of the cheques paid in and not given credit for in the Pass Book, and the result should be a balance identical with that shown in the Pass Book.

The Auditor must use his own discretion, guided Examination of the Subsidiary Books. by his experience, as to how far it may be necessary to check the details found in the Subsidiary Books. As previously stated, he should make as much use as possible of documents obtained from independent sources to guard against errors of omission.

When once an entry of any transaction is made in the books it may be said to come under the cognisance of the Auditor, and a perfect balance can only be obtained by each of these entries being carried forward, step by step, into the Ledger. The Auditor has, however, to guard against their being carried to a wrong Ledger Account, and also any other inaccuracies in the posting.

CHAPTER VI.

FORMS OF ACCOUNTS PUBLISHED BY COMPANIES.

Variety in Forms of Accounts published by Companies—Some prescribed by Act of Parliament—Balance Sheet prescribed by Companies Act, 1862, Table A—Forms prescribed by Life Assurance Companies Act, 1870—By Regulation of Railways Act, 1868—By Gasworks Clauses Act, 1847—By Metropolis Water Act, 1862—Revenue Account and Balance Sheet usually issued alone when Forms not prescribed— Statement of Receipts and Expenditure or Cash Account— Difference between Revenue Account and Cash Account— Receipts and Expenditure Account should show total Receipts and Expenditure to Date—Balance Sheet—The Statements which afford the Shareholders all the requisite Information.

Variety in Forms of Accounts published by Companies. THE Accounts of Public Companies, as placed before their Auditors for confirmation, vary very considerably. In some Companies the forms are specially prescribed, and are set forth in Schedules to the Acts of Parliament under which they work, while other Companies are unfettered in this respect, and it is left entirely to their officers as to how the results of their management are laid before the Shareholders.

Life Assurance, Railway (including Tramway) and Gas Companies, are examples of the first class, while nearly all Companies registered under the Companies Act, 1862, are at liberty to use their own forms of Accounts, with the exception of those registered without Articles of Association.

These Companies are required to present their Balance Sheet in the form annexed to the first Schedule of that Act, or as near thereto as circumstances admit. *Balance Sheet prescribed by Companies Act, 1862, Table A.*

The Accounts of Life Assurance Companies, registered under the Act of 1862, as many are, are, like all other Life Assurance Companies, subject to the forms prescribed by the Life Assurance Companies Act, 1870, and which have to be filed annually with the Board of Trade. *Forms prescribed by Life Assurance Companies Act, 1870*

Railway Companies are compelled, by the Regulation of Railways Act, 1868, to publish, in addition to the Revenue Account and Balance Sheet prescribed by that Act, five statements relating to their Capital, showing with details the Capital authorised and created by the Company, the proportion received, the Capital raised by Loans and Debenture Stock, and the receipts and expenditure on Capital Account; they are also compelled by the same Act to publish two statements relating to the estimated further expenditure on Capital Account, a return of Working Stock, and two mileage statements. *By Regulation of Railways Act, 1868.*

Gas Companies are required by the Gas Works Clauses Act, 1847, Amendment, to publish detailed statements of their Share and Loan Capital. *By Gas Works Clauses Act, 1847.*

The Metropolis Water Act, 1862, enacts that the Metropolitan Water Works Companies shall prepare an Account of the total receipts and expen- *By Metropolis Water Act.*

diture of all Rates or other moneys levied under the powers of their Act under the several distinct heads of Receipts and Expenditure.

The Accounts just referred to, and all other similar statements, are statistical, and do not form part of the Book-keeping proper.

Revenue Account and Balance Sheet usually issued alone when Form not prescribed. The Accounts of those Companies which are at liberty to present them in their own forms are usually set forth in two statements, a Revenue or Profit and Loss Account, and a statement of Liabilities and Assets, generally known as a Balance Sheet.

The result of the Book-keeping culminates in these two statements, and it is to the investigation of these the attention of the Auditor is principally confined. Any other statements which may be brought under his notice are abstracts from the Cash Book, compiled for the purpose of showing how a particular class of receipt has been expended.

With one exception they require no comment, both the preparation of these statements and checking their correctness being a mere mechanical process.

Statement of Receipts and Expenditure or Cash Account. The exception just referred to, is a general statement of Receipts and Expenditure or abstract of the Cash Account, which is frequently published by Companies in addition to a Revenue Account and Balance Sheet, and in some instances it is substituted for a Revenue Account and issued to the Shareholders, in conjunction with a Balance Sheet alone. This Cash Account of course shows the Shareholders how their Capital and the other receipts of the Company have been expended or invested, and if the Debtors of the Company discharged their obligations by prompt payment, on the completion of each transaction, and if the Company, on the other hand, settled with their Creditors in the same manner, this Account, together with a Balance Sheet, would be the only statement required for laying before the Shareholders the result of the business of the period.

Public Companies, however, almost without exception, take advantage of credit, and, on the other hand, are obliged, in transacting business with their customers, to afford them the same facilities, consequently a Cash Account does not convey to the Shareholders all the information requisite to show the result of the transactions of the Company.

The difference therefore between a Cash Account and Revenue Account is that the former is merely a summary of the Cash received and expended, as stated in detail in the Cash Book, while the latter shows on the one side the total income of the period, irrespective of whether the same has been actually received or is due to the Company, and on the other side the total outgoings or charge, without taking into consideration, with the exception of allowances for depreciation or for bad and doubtful debts, whether the same has been paid, or is owing by the Company.

All·receipts and payments relating to Capital, and not to Income, would be omitted in the Revenue Account, but would of course have to be included in the Cash Account; for example: The following items appearing in the Cash Account would therefore be omitted in the Revenue Account for the same period. On the Income side, Shareholders'

Capital, Premium on Shares issued, Amount received on Mortgage and on Loan, or on the Sale of Securities; and on the other side, Sums paid for the purchase of Securities, Sums advanced on Mortgage or in repayment of Mortgages, and Sums advanced on Loans, or the amount of Loans repaid.

On the other hand, the following items would appear in a Revenue Account which would be absent in a Cash Account. On the Income side Sales not paid for at the date of closing the Books, Interest on Investments accrued, but not received; while on the Expenditure side would be found purchases by the Company not paid for, and other similar entries.

Receipts and Expenditure Account should show total Receipts and Expenditure to Date. The Receipts and Expenditure Account should show not only the receipts and expenditure of the period, but also the total amount of Cash received, and the total expenditure from the commencement of the Company's existence.

Balance Sheet. The other statement, issued to the Shareholders in conjunction with the Revenue Account, is one of Liabilities and Assets, usually known as a Balance Sheet. This Document shows on the one side the Capital of the Company, both Share and Loan, the amount due to Creditors, and any other liabilities of the Company arranged under the proper headings, while on the other side are enumerated the Assets and property.

The three Statements which afford full Information to the Shareholders. The "Receipts and Expenditure Account," "Revenue Account," and "Balance Sheet," can therefore afford the Shareholders full information respecting the affairs of their undertaking. From the first statement they can ascertain how their Capital and Cash receipts from all sources have been expended. The second gives the result of the operations for the period over which it extends, while the third shows the financial position their transactions have resulted in.

The first of these statements has been already explained as being an abstract of the Cash Book. The other two will be found treated in the following chapters.

CHAPTER VII.

THE REVENUE ACCOUNT.

Explanation of the Revenue Account—Difference between Revenue Account and Cash Account—Trading Account— Profit and Loss Account—Best Method of stating a Revenue Account—Stock in hand at commencement of the Period—Purchases—Claims under Policies—Interest on Debentures—Interest on Mortgages—Amount written off Leasehold Property—Royalties—Dead Rent—Expenses of Management—Resolution of the Council of the Institute of Actuaries—Directors' Fees—Salaries—Wages—Commission —Rent, Rates, Taxes, &c.—Repairs and Renewals—Amount written off for Depreciation—Loss on Realisation of Securities—Debts irrecoverable—Amount written off Preliminary Expenses—Interest to Shareholders—Auditor should resist proposal to pay Dividends out of Capital—Income side of the Revenue Account—Sales—Premiums—Interest on Investments—Transfer Fees—Traffic and other Receipts-- Stock in hand at end of the Period—Premiums on Shares —Balance of the Revenue Account.

Explanation of the Revenue Account.

THE Revenue Account, also called a Profit and Loss Account, is, as its latter name implies, a statement showing either how the profit has been earned or the loss sustained on the operations of the Company for the period brought under the notice of the Auditor.

The title Revenue Account is a better one than that of Profit and Loss, as the latter is somewhat misleading—the items comprehending the legitimate expenses and charges incidental to carrying on the business being placed on the same side as the losses.

The difference between a Revenue Account and a Cash Account has already been explained, but it may be here stated that whereas the latter only shows the actual amount of cash received and paid away, the former shows, on the credit side, the income or the earnings, irrespective of whether the same has been actually received, or at the date of closing the books is due to the Company, while, on the other or debit side are set forth the expenses, irrespective of whether they have been paid or are owing by the Company at the same date.

Difference between Revenue Account and Cash Account.

The balance of these two sides, therefore, shows whether the transactions of the period have resulted in a profit or a loss according as the credit side or the debit side is respectively the greater.

The Revenue Account of a trading Company usually comprehends the two statements known among accountants as a Trading Account and a Profit and Loss Account. The former shows the gross profit or the gross loss of the period, being the difference between the amount of stock in hand at the commencement of the period, purchases, wages, and other expenses incidental to production, as against the sales and the stock in hand at the end of the period.

Trading Account.

The balance of this account is carried forward to the Profit and Loss Account, and is then charged with the general expenses incidental to carrying on the business. The balance, after bringing in these

Profit and Loss Account.

charges, shows the actual or net profit, or the loss, of the period.

Best method of stating a Revenue Account. The best method, therefore, of stating the Revenue Account of a Company is to divide it into three sections, the first showing in the same manner as a trading account the gross profit or loss, the second resulting in a net profit or loss (as the case may be) of the period, while in the third should be set forth, as explained hereafter, the balance of this and previous Revenue Accounts, and the dividends paid to Shareholders, resulting in an actual surplus or deficiency, to date of the transactions of the Company.

It would be quite impossible to discuss in detail every description of income and expenditure which could possibly come under the notice of an Auditor, for as almost every class of business is registered under the various Joint-Stock Companies Acts, such may almost be said to be innumerable. The most familiar headings, however, which occur in the Revenue Accounts of Companies are treated in the present chapter, the remarks on one or more of which will afford assistance to an Auditor requiring information as to how an item of receipt or expenditure, not included here, should be treated.

Stock in hand at commencement of the period. Commencing with the debit side of the Revenue Account. In all trading Companies the first heading is usually the Stock in hand at the commencement of the period which comes under the investigation of the Auditor.

In the case of a new Company this item will not, of course, appear; and when a Company has previously published a Revenue Account, the duty of

the Auditor is confined to merely ascertaining that
the figures coincide with those under the heading of
" Stock in hand " at the date on which the previous
Revenue Account was made up to. Unless, therefore, he audited the accounts for the preceding
period he is not answerable for the accuracy of the
amount, that responsibility rests with the Auditor
who signed the previous accounts.

The figures as certified by him and adopted by the
Shareholders at their meeting cannot be afterwards
altered; but should the Auditor ascertain that any
figures in the previous accounts are inaccurate, he
should either require a correcting entry made in the
accounts he is auditing, or else he should call attention to the fact in his report, as an explanation why
the apparent profit or loss, as the case may be, has
been unduly increased or diminished by the inaccu-
racy of the previous accounts presented to the
Shareholders.

The item naturally coming after the stock-in-trade Purchases.
is that representing the additions made to it during
the period embraced by the Revenue Account. The
single word " Purchases " is the usual heading under
which is included the cost of the goods purchased
which are intended to be resold at a profit. The
amounts paid for plant, machinery, office furniture,
&c., necessary for the purpose of carrying on the
business, do not appear in the Revenue Account.

In accordance with the theory (already explained)
on which the Revenue Account is prepared, it is, of
course, immaterial whether the goods purchased had
been paid for at the date of closing the books or

were still owing for. The total amount has to be included under " Purchases," and the amounts outstanding will be found among the liabilities in the Balance Sheet under the heading " Creditors."

Claims under Policies. In Insurance Companies of every description, life, fire, accident, marine, guarantee, &c., the principal charge against the Revenue Accounts consists of the " Claims " under its Policies, and in dealing with this item the Auditor has to be careful that not only those Claims which have been made during the period, and in respect of which the stipulated amount of compensation has been paid, are included under this heading, but also those in addition that had been notified to the office.

He may, however, at his discretion, allow a deduction to be made in respect of any Claims which the Company do not admit themselves liable to pay, and which they intend to resist. The opinion of the Company's Solicitor would be of assistance to the Auditor in determining the amount to be thus deducted.

All amounts included under the above heading, which had not been paid at the date on which the Books were closed, must, of course, be brought into the Balance Sheet as a liability.

Interest on Debentures. When a Company has borrowed money on Debentures the holders of these Debentures are creditors of the Company, and therefore the interest payable to them must be kept distinct from that paid to the Shareholders, which represents payment on account of profits.

The former must be charged against the Revenue

Account before the profits, out of which Dividends can only properly be paid, are ascertained. The interest paid to the Debenture holders is not dependent on profits, and the rate per cent. is arranged at the time of issuing the Debentures.

The same remarks are applicable to the Interest payable to those who have advanced money to the Company on ordinary mortgage of its property. *Interest on Mortgages.*

When Leasehold Property forms part of the assets of a Company the Auditor should be satisfied that a sufficient portion has been written off each Lease and charged against the Revenue Account, so that a proportionate decrease takes place each year in the amount standing as the value of each Lease in the books of the Company until its expiration. *Amount written off Leasehold Property.*

Leasehold Property may be held by a Company either as an investment or for occupation. In either case the above remark applies, while the rents received from the investment, after deducting the incidental expenses, such as law costs, repairs, rates, taxes, &c., should be included among the income. When a Company occupies its own Leasehold premises, the proportion written off is equivalent to a rent, and should be treated accordingly.

A Table for calculating the amount to be set aside annually in order to exhaust a Lease will be found in the Appendix, with directions explaining how it is to be used, also an example in the form of a Ledger Account showing how a Lease is gradually exhausted in this manner The interest calculated on each balance brought down and debited to the Lease Account is, of course, taken credit for in the

Revenue Account among "Interest on Investments."

Royalties. The Revenue Account of Mining Companies should be charged by the Royalties payable in respect of all minerals sold during the period **Dead Rent.** under Audit. Any Dead Rent for the same period should also be charged against the Revenue Account, but the Auditor may allow the Company to take credit among its assets for any Dead Rent so charged which it is expected will be recouped out of Royalties before the limit of time allowed for that purpose in the Lease will have expired.

Expenses of Management. With reference to the Expenses of Management, it is usual in large Companies to place Directors' Fees, Salaries, Wages, and General Office Expenses, under one head, but in small Companies they are generally set forth in detail in the Revenue Account.

In either case the Auditor should be equally careful to ascertain that all the expenses are included. As already explained it does not affect the amount, which should be here set forth, whether all the items have been actually paid or not, settled or still owing, they must all be charged against the Revenue Account.

Very often an attempt is made, especially in the first Revenue Account of a Company, to omit certain charges on the ground that they have not been paid, or that the exact amounts are not known or have not been agreed upon. This the Auditor should strenuously resist, and should defer the completion of the Accounts until the doubtful amounts have been ascertained or a satisfactory estimate has been

made, and the amount included in the Revenue
Account.

With reference to the Revenue Accounts of Life Resolution of the Council
Assurance Companies, the following Resolution was of the Institute of
passed at a meeting of the Council of the Institute Actuaries.
of Actuaries in consequence of an inquiry made of
them by the Board of Trade :

" That in the opinion of the Council, every
" expense, of whatever kind, incurred by a Life
" Assurance Company for the purpose of promoting,
" carrying on, or extending the business of the
" Company, should, with the exception of Commis-
" sion, be included under the head of ' Expenses of
" Management ' in the accounts registered in con-
" formity with the Act."

The following remarks on the various expenses
incidental to the conduct of the business of public
Companies are equally applicable whether they are
set forth in detail in the Revenue Account or are
embraced under one comprehensive heading, such
as, for example, " Expenses of Management."

It has just been remarked that very frequently in
preparing the first Revenue Account of a Company
the officials, in order to make it appear as favorable
as possible, leave out charges on the ground they
have not been paid, or perhaps even not ascertained ;
this is especially applicable to Directors' fees.

Now, on the principle previously laid down that a Directors' Fees.
Revenue Account is a statement of the actual in-
come and expenditure of the period, and not of
receipts and payments, this explanation should not
be considered satisfactory by the Auditor ; and

8

unless the Board actually pass a resolution at one of their meetings, which is entered in the minute book in the usual way, that they do not intend to receive any remuneration for their services to the date on which the accounts are made up, the Auditor should require some sum to be inserted.

Amount sometimes settled by Private Act or Articles of Association.

Sometimes the amount of the remuneration of the Directors is fixed by the Private Acts or Articles of Association, which may be either a stated sum or a commission on the sales, income, gross profit or net profit, &c., or even a combination of these. When this is the case it is easy to determine the amount to be charged in the accounts, and if the Directors have not received it they must be included among the creditors of the Company in the Balance Sheet for the sums due to them respectively.

Sometimes left to Shareholders.

Frequently the remuneration of the Directors is left in the hands of the Shareholders, to be voted at their general meeting. It is then, however, usually arranged previously what amount the Shareholders will vote, in which case it may be inserted. In any event, however, when the actual sum is not known, an estimated amount should be charged against the Revenue Account, which, although only approximate, must be certainly more accurate than omitting the item altogether.

Salaries.

The remuneration of the Secretary, Manager, Clerks, and other officials on the regular staff of the Company, is usually included in one sum among the outgo of the Revenue Account, under the heading " Salaries," and should be kept distinct from the

Wages.

sums paid as wages to workmen, artisans, mechanics,

and others whose remuneration is contingent on the quantity of work done, and fluctuates accordingly.

Directors' fees should never be included with the salaries, but the fixed remuneration of a Managing Director always should be unless stated separately.

Frequently a Manager and other officials are paid entirely by a Commission, or are allowed, in addition to their fixed salary, a Commission on the amount of the business done by the Company or in a particular department. In either case the Commission should never be included under the heading of " Salaries." The amount should either be added to " Commission " or else stated by itself.

When a bonus is given to the officials the amount should either be stated separately or the heading should be extended to " Salaries including bonuses to officials." This remark applies to any pensions paid to retired officials of the Company.

When Commission is paid, for influencing sales, or Commission. any description of income, the amount so allowed should either be stated by itself or else (except in the Revenue Accounts of Companies transacting Insurance business) included in the general heading, " Expenses of Management."

Commission should never be deducted from the sales, or from any other source of income, for securing which the Commission is allowed.

The amount stated in the Revenue Account must consist not only of the Commission which has been actually paid, but must also include any which will have to be paid on the income taken credit for in this account. To ascertain this sum precisely is often a troublesome task for the Auditor, as frequently attempts are made to understate the amount of Commission which has not been actually paid in order to increase the apparent profits.

When an agent or traveller has received money in advance to be deducted from Commission expected to be earned by him in the future, that portion only which has been earned on income taken credit for in the Revenue Account should be charged. The balance should be treated as an ordinary cash advance, and the agent should be included among the debtors on the asset side of the Balance Sheet for the unearned portion of the Commission.

The Auditor should ascertain that the Commission has not been participated in by any person acting in a fiduciary capacity towards the Company, unless this is expressly provided for in the Special Acts of Parliament or in the Articles of Association. This remark applies also to brokerage for placing Share Capital, Debentures, &c.

Rent, Rates, Taxes, &c.
Under the heading of " Rent, Rates, Taxes, &c.," should be included the Rent of all offices and premises on which the business of the Company is transacted, together with the Rates and Taxes incidental thereto, but it should not include the Rent paid for premises which are sublet to other tenants.

In other words, when only a portion of the premises of which the Company are tenants are used by it as their place of business, and the remainder is sublet, there should only be included under the heading " Rent, &c.," the difference between the Rent paid by the Company and that received from its subtenants. It would, therefore, be wrong to put the Rents received from the Company's subtenants of their actual business premises on the income side of the Revenue Account, and the entire Rent paid for the premises on the expenditure side. The heading "Rent, Rates, and Taxes," consequently refers only to those amounts which might be included under the heading "Expenses of Management."

The amount which ought to be charged against the Revenue Account of Companies possessing Plant, Machinery, Buildings, &c., for repairs, frequently requires very careful attention by the Auditor.

Repairs and Renewals.

Unless a Company is in a very flourishing condition, there is a great tendency to add to the amount standing in the Books as representing the value of these Assets, those sums which have actually been expended in repairing or replacing part of them, and which ought therefore to be included in the expenditure side of the Revenue Account under "Repairs and Renewals," or some similar heading.

This the Auditor must not allow, the necessary buildings having been erected, and the plant and machinery purchased, the Accounts representing the expenditure thereon should be closed, and no additions permitted. Should the business, however, increase, and additional buildings and machinery become necessary, the further expenditure on this account may, of course, be treated as an Asset, but the whole of the money laid out for keeping them in order must be charged against the Revenue Accounts.

In exceptional cases, as for example, if the sum expended on repairs and renewals be very heavy in any one year, and the Auditor is satisfied it will suffice for the next two or three years, he may, at his discretion, allow the amount to be placed to a separate Account, and only charge one half or one third against the Revenue Account for the ensuing two or three years.

Amount written off for Depreciation. The Auditor should also require a proper amount written off for depreciation of plant, machinery, &c. This is usually a percentage on the cost, and small or large according as it has to be seldom or frequently replaced, the object being to charge the Revenue Account of the period with a proper sum for the usage of the plant, and for the balance to represent its present value.

In many Companies it is the practice to add the sums periodically expended on the purchase of new machinery to the General Plant Account, and to write off a fixed percentage on the balance against each Revenue Account. To this plan the Auditor cannot raise any objection, provided he is satisfied the balance of the Account is not in excess of the value.

Loss on Realisation of Securities. Should a loss be sustained by the Company on the realisation of any of its Capital invested on Mortgage or any class of securities, the amount should be distinctly stated in the Revenue Account, and not be concealed by being included in any item of expenditure.

Debts irrecoverable. When there are many Ledger Accounts there is almost certain to be a loss on the realisation of the outstanding balances due to the Company, as it is practically impossible for any extensive business to be carried on without bad debts being occasionally incurred.

An Auditor cannot of course be expected to be acquainted with, or even to ascertain the financial position of those he may find by the Books are indebted to the Company, but it is clearly part of his duty to take all reasonable means to prevent the Company taking credit for sums appearing by the Books to be due to it, the whole of which it is certain will not be eventually received.

He should therefore have prepared for him a list of all those who were indebted to the Company at the date on which the Books were closed, and this he should go through carefully with the official who, in his opinion, is the one most likely to be acquainted with the financial position of these Debtors.

It is a very convenient plan to have a list prepared for him, classifying the Debtors under three headings, namely good, doubtful, and bad. The amount due from the first may of course be fully taken credit for among the Assets, and with regard to the doubtful debts only a percentage such as 60, 75, or 90 per cent. of the total amount should be assumed as likely to be eventually received, while the balance of 40, 25, or 10 per cent., together with the total of the debts returned as bad, should be charged against the Revenue Account as " Debts irrecoverable," or under some similar heading.

When a Company employs agents the balances due from them at the end of the period under audit may be treated in the same manner.

In many Companies it is usual to write off a small percentage, such as one or one and a half per cent., on the sales, and charge that amount against the

Revenue Account as a provision for losses estimated to arise on realisation. When, however, this plan is adopted the Auditor must be careful that the rate per cent. is sufficiently high. Even then it is not so satisfactory a way of determining the amount which ought to be written off as an allowance for bad debts as in going through the list of debtors seriatim, and treating the balances in the manner recommended above.

Amount written off Preliminary Expenses.

The expenses incurred in the formation of a Company are usually brought together into a suspense account called " Preliminary Expenses," and as it would be unfair towards the business of the first year to charge the whole amount against its Revenue Account, it is the recognised custom to write off a proportion, such as one fifth, against the Revenue Account of the first five years, at the end of which time this suspense account would thus be extinguished.

This method of dealing with the Preliminary Expenses Account is frequently provided for in the Special Act or the Articles of Association, but when that has not been done the arrangement is perfectly legitimate, and may be permitted by the Auditor. The number of years, however, over which the " Preliminary Expenses " Account may extend should, if not provided for in the Special Act or Articles of Association, as a rule, not exceed five or six, except in very special cases, for which ten should be the extreme limit permitted.

Interest paid to Shareholders.

It is the custom with many Companies to place the " Interest paid to Shareholders " in the Revenue

Account among the Expenditure. This is very incorrect, and should be objected to by the Auditor. The Revenue Account should show clearly the actual or net profit, out of which a dividend can be paid, or if no profit has been earned the fact should be distinctly shown.

If, notwithstanding that a loss has been sustained during the period to which the accounts refer, a dividend be paid to the Shareholders, the Revenue Account should show at a glance that it is paid either out of past profits or that its payment creates or adds to a previous deficiency, in other words, is paid out of the Shareholders' Capital.

In order that these desirable facts may be properly set forth, the Revenue Account should be divided into two sections, the first (which may be subdivided as previously suggested) consisting exclusively of the actual income and expenditure of the period under audit, the balance of which, showing the net profit or the actual loss, should be carried down to the second part of the Revenue Account.

Revenue Account should be divided into two Sections.

In this second part should also be set forth the balance brought forward from the previous Revenue Account (if any) representing the undivided profits or the deficiency at that date, also the amount of the interest or dividend proposed to be paid to the Shareholders. Any interim dividend paid to the Shareholders since the last accounts were made up, and any bonus proposed to be distributed among the Shareholders, should be entered in the second part of the Revenue Account, which should also include the Reserve Fund (if any), and any additions made to it during the period.

This supplementary statement therefore shows clearly out of what funds the proposed dividend would have to be paid, whether out of the profits of the period, or partly or wholly out of the past profits, or partly or wholly out of the Capital of the Company.

Auditor should remonstrate against Payment of Dividends out of Capital.
It is clearly the duty of the Auditor to resist the proposal to pay a Dividend to the Shareholders out of their own Capital, and should the Directors persist in their intention of doing so he should, in his Report to the Shareholders, clearly state that no Dividend has been legitimately earned, and that he disapproves of the proposal of the Directors.

The Shareholders then have the opportunity at their Meeting of refusing to sanction the declaration of a Dividend, should they resolve on receiving one they alone are responsible for the consequences, and if the withdrawal of the Capital required for paying the Dividend leads to unfortunate results, they cannot in any way blame their Auditor.

Income side of the Revenue Account.
The Income side of the Revenue Account contains the amount of the Revenue derived from the business, for carrying on which the Company was established, together with that of any additional and incidental Income.

Sales.
In trading Companies the principal source of revenue consists of that derived from Sales, which may be classed under three heads :

(1.) Sales for Cash.

(2.) Sales on Credit, paid for before the closing of the books.

(3.) Sales on Credit, unpaid at the date of closing the books.

The two first items do not require any comment, but the third demands the most careful consideration of the Auditor, as therefrom may arise bad debts. The best way of ascertaining how much should be charged against the Revenue Account to provide for the probable failure of some of the debtors of the Company to meet their engagements to it has already been shown, and it is only necessary to add that the sum decided upon should always be entered on the debit side of the Revenue Account, and never be deducted from the amount of the Sales. In other words, the amounts debited to customers for goods sold to them must be set forth in full in one sum on the Income side of the Revenue Account, while any bad debts or losses expected to arise on the realisation of the balances must be distinctly stated on the other side of the Account.

The value of any goods returned by purchasers should be deducted from the sales, but this is the only exception, the total amount, therefore, of the sales, after deducting the value of the goods returned, should be brought into the income side of the Revenue Account, while all charges and expenses connected with influencing such Sales should be set forth on the debit side. In no other way can the Shareholders see the total amount of the business done, and the expenses incurred in transacting it.

Returned Goods.

Premiums.   The principal source of Income of all Companies
transacting insurance business, whether life, fire,
marine, accident, guarantee, &c., is the Premiums
they receive for undertaking the risk of the insurance.

In auditing the Revenue Account of an Insurance
Company the Auditor must be careful that only
those Premiums are taken credit for which fall due
in the period under audit. Premiums paid in
advance falling due after the date of closing the
books should not be taken credit for, but they
should be brought into the Balance Sheet among
the liabilities, and would form part of the Income
in the following Revenue Account.

It therefore follows that Premiums received
during the period under audit, but which fell due
previously, should not be included, as they, of
course, belong to the preceding period. In the
event, however, of their not having then been taken
credit for they should be added to the amount of
funds at the beginning of the year, with a note
explaining their previous omission.

The Auditor must ascertain that Note 2 of the
first Schedule of the Life Assurance Companies Act,
1870, has been attended to.

This Note prescribes that the amounts paid and
received in respect of reassurances should be deducted from the Premiums, and not charged against
the Revenue Account on the other side.

When part of a Premium is allowed to remain on
credit the whole Premium should be included among
the Income, and the part not paid should be in-

cluded among the Assets, under the heading " Loans
on Company's Policies."

The Interest and Dividends received on the In- Interest on
Investments
vestments of a Company, so far as they relate to the
period since the date on which the books were last
closed, or if the Company be a new one, since its
incorporation, must be taken credit for in the
Revenue Account, and in addition, the Interest
accrued to the date of closing the books.

For example, supposing the books are made up
at the 31st December, and one of the Company's
Investments are Bank Stock, the Dividends on which
are paid on the 5th April and 5th October in each
year, the proportion of Interest for the period between
the 5th October and the 31st December should be
taken credit for, of course supposing the Investment
to have been made prior to the 6th October, otherwise the proportion only can be taken credit for.

When the Shares of another Company are held as Shares in
other
an Investment, the accrued Interest can only be Companies.
estimated, as the rate of Dividend which will be
declared cannot, of course, be known. The Auditor
must, however, not allow too sanguine an estimate
to be assumed.

The Interest derived from Investments in Debentures of a Company, or from Mortgages, being fixed,
the calculation can be easily made.

Another source of Revenue in nearly all Com- Transfer
Fees.
panies is the Fees received for the Registration of the
Transfer of Shares, usually called " Transfer Fees."
In those Companies whose Shares are not quoted in
the official list of the Stock Exchange the income

received from this source is generally trifling, but in large Companies in whose Shares there is constant speculation, the Transfer Fees often form an appreciable item of Revenue.

Traffic and other Receipts.

The Revenues of Railway, Tramway, Omnibus, and similar Companies, consist mainly of Receipts for the conveyance of passengers and goods. Banks and Discount Companies derive theirs principally from discounting Mercantile Bills. Gas and Waterworks' Companies from the rates they charge for the consumption of their respective supplies. These demand no special directions for the guidance of the Auditor. He must, of course, be careful to ascertain that no amounts are taken credit for which have not been properly earned, and that when it is necessary to make an estimate it has been done on a reasonable and moderate basis.

Stock in hand at end of the Period.

At the commencement of this chapter it was remarked that the debit side of the Revenue Account of a trading Company commenced with the Stock in hand at the beginning of the period, and consequently the credit side will include the value of the Stock left in the possession of the Company at the date on which the books are closed, that is, of the unsold portion of the purchases of the period, and perhaps of the Stock in hand included in the debit side of the Account.

The Auditor cannot, of course, be held responsible for the value assigned to this Stock; he should, however, satisfy himself that due allowance has been made for depreciation, which varies greatly according to the nature of the Stock.

The Auditor should also ascertain as far as possible that the Stock has been properly taken, and require its being certified to that effect by the Manager or some other responsible officer of the Company.

If the Stock is believed not to have decreased in value, it is usual to insert in the Revenue Account the amount at cost price, in which case it is as well to state that fact.

In different trades the mode of procedure in taking the Stock varies, but the object of doing so is, of course, to ascertain (by number, quantity, measurement, or weight) the value of the entire Stock-in-trade, that is, the unsold portion of the goods purchased for the purpose of their being sold again.

When a Company carrying on a successful business requires additional Capital for the purpose of extending its transactions, it is a very general practice to issue the new Shares at a Premium. *Premiums on Shares.*

There are many reasons for this, one being that when the market value of the Shares of a Company are above par it would depreciate this value were the new Shares issued below it. Another reason is, that it would not be fair to the Shareholders, who have borne the risk of establishing and bringing the Company to its flourishing condition, for others to come in and share their reward without giving them some equivalent for the privilege.

These premiums should not be brought into the Revenue Account, but should be invested and placed to the credit of the " Reserve Fund," or, if there be none, should form the commencement of one. The *Should not be brought into Revenue Account.*

amount may, however, with great propriety be applied towards the liquidation of a fictitious Asset Account such as that of " Preliminary Expenses."

When the profits are not sufficiently large to admit of a dividend being paid out of them, and the Directors in distributing one have recourse to the " Reserve Fund," the amount taken therefrom should not be included among the income shown in the Revenue Account.

As previously remarked, this statement should show the actual profit or loss of the period, and it would not do so if amounts of this description were improperly added to the income instead of being brought into the supplementary statement previously explained and recommended.

Balance of the Revenue Account. The final Balance of the Revenue Account representing the amount of undivided profits or the deficiency resulting from either mismanagement or misfortune is transferred to the Balance Sheet, where it remains, showing, in conjunction with the other entries therein, the financial position of the Company.

CHAPTER VIII.

THE BALANCE SHEET.

Explanation of the Balance Sheet—Should be carefully examined by the Auditor—Liabilities—Capital—Preference Shares—Debentures—Railway Debentures—Creditors—Amount due to Mortgagees—Liability on Bills Receivable Discounted—Shareholders' Interest outstanding—Claims admitted but not paid—Amount due on Current and Deposit Accounts—Reserve—Reserve Fund—Balance of Revenue Account (Surplus)—Assets—Government Securities—Shares and Debentures in Joint Stock Companies—Investments should stand in Names of the Trustees—Freehold and Leasehold Property—Mortgages—Loans—Debtors—Bills Receivable on hand—Agents' Balances—Company's own Shares—Interest on Investments due and accrued—Cash—Stock-in-Trade—Office Furniture—Purchase of Business, &c.—Purchases on Hiring Agreements—Preliminary Expenses—Balance of Revenue Account (Deficiency)—Balance Sheet should be so explicit as to be understood by every Shareholder.

THE Balance Sheet may certainly be said to be the most important statement of any which can be laid before the Shareholders, as, if properly drawn up, it shows the exact financial position of the Company.

On one side are placed the liabilities, not only to the Creditors, but also to the Partners or Shareholders themselves, while on the other side are

Explanation of the Balance Sheet.

9

enumerated the assets and the property of the Company.

Before giving his certificate to the correctness of this statement the Auditor must examine in detail each item on both sides, and satisfy himself that the liabilities have not been understated nor the assets overestimated, as, without intending to deceive the Shareholders, or to act in any way dishonestly, it is quite possible for the Directors and Officials of a Company to present the Balance Sheet in a more favorable light than is warranted by the facts.

It must not be overlooked that, while it would be very improper for the Directors to intentionally deceive their Co-partners in any particular, yet in many instances it would be very unfair to themselves and to the Shareholders, as well as very impolitic, to either overstate the liabilities or to underestimate the assets.

This applies to Companies whose business depends on their periodically showing to their constituents and the public their sound and unquestionable financial position, for while, on the one hand, nothing could be more reprehensible than for the Directors of a Bank to deceive their Shareholders and the customers, by stating its securities at a value they know they do not possess, yet they would naturally, as competitors for public patronage, desire to set forth the assets at their fair market value, and to this the Auditor cannot raise any objection. As a matter of prudence, however, he might suggest the cost price being inserted in the Balance Sheet, supposing the securities have not depreciated in value, and it being stated, in a foot-note, the actual market value at the date on which the Balance Sheet is made out.

The Liabilities as shown in a Company's Balance Liabilities. Sheet may be classed under two heads :

(1.) Liabilities to the Shareholders.

(2.) Liabilities to the Public.

The former consists of the Capital, which may be Capital. represented either by Stock or Shares. If the latter, the Shares may be either all of one equal value, or some may be of larger amount than others. Again, the Shares may either entitle their holders to receive an equal share of the profits, or some of them may confer the right to a Preferential Dividend, either at the same rate of interest, or perhaps at a higher or a lower rate, than the " Ordinary " Shares, the former usually being known by that name, the latter being usually styled " Preference " Shares.

There are two classes of Preference Shares, one Preference Shares. which entitles their holders to a Preferential Dividend out of the profits of the year only, the other which claims the Preferential Dividend out of the profits of preceding or future years, in the event of the profits of any one year being not sufficient to provide for the stipulated interest.

Unless, however, it is expressly provided for in the Private Act or Articles of Association, Prefer-ence Shareholders are only entitled to the Prefer-ential Dividend out of the profits of each year, and if there are not profits available for the payment of the full amount no part of the deficiency can be made good out of the profits of any subsequent year or out of any other funds of the Company.

Details of the Capital should be set out. The Details showing the particulars of the Capital should be clearly stated, and when it is divided into more than one class of Shares this should be shown, also the number of Shares authorised to be issued either by the Special Act of Parliament or the Memorandum of Association, the number actually issued, the total nominal value of the Shares issued, and the amount paid up. Any sums paid in advance of calls should also be stated.

Debentures. In addition to the Stock or Shares there is another class of Capital frequently made use of by Companies, technically known as " Debenture Capital." This, as its name implies, is borrowed Capital, the repayment of which may be secured to the lenders by a mortgage deed either on part or on the whole of the property of the Company.

Railway Debentures. Railway Debentures made in the form given in Schedule C of the Companies Clauses Consolidation Act, 1845, are only secured on the tolls and earnings of the undertaking and not on the capital, the permanent way, the rolling stock, or any part of the railway itself.

Debenture holders are, of course, creditors of the Company, but the amount due to them should be kept distinct from the sums due to ordinary creditors. In a few Companies they have the privilege of voting at meetings, also of having their own Auditor.

Sundry Creditors. Under "Sundry Creditors" or some similar heading should be included all the sums due to those Creditors of the Company who are not Debenture holders and who do not hold security for the payment of the same. The amounts due to Debenture holders, whether they do or do not possess security, and to mortgagees of the Company's property, should not consequently be included under this heading.

It, therefore, follows that only the sums due to two classes of Creditors can be here set out, namely, those on Bills of Exchange Payable, and those on open accounts, and the amounts due to each class is usually stated.

Great care should be taken by the Auditor to ensure that all of the latter class are included. It is not, however, the omission of the amounts due to those Creditors who supply the Company with goods, which are either sold again or manufactured into other goods for resale, that he has to guard against; they are almost invariably entered in the books as soon as they reach the Company's premises. The difficulty is to ensure that among the liabilities under the above heading are included all the sums due to Creditors chargeable against the Revenue Account and which should be included in the expenses. The accounts representing these are frequently not sent in until some time after the books are closed and are in consequence omitted.

The amount of the liability to those who have advanced money to the Company secured by a Mortgage on some or the whole of its property should be included among the liabilities under a separate heading, such as " Amount due to Mortgagees." The amount set out should be that of the sums actually advanced to the Company; any

Amount due to Mortgagees.

accrued or outstanding interest thereon should be included with other amounts due to creditors, or if in arrear should be stated separately.

Liability on Bills Receivable Discounted. When Bills of Exchange Receivable come into the possession of a Company from any of its debtors they are either retained by the Company until they become due, or they are discounted and the proceeds made use of for business purposes.

In the latter case, should the acceptor of a Bill become insolvent before it falls due, and it is not in consequence honored on presentation, the discounter will look to the Company to refund him the proceeds.

The Auditor should therefore go carefully through the list of the Bills Receivable which have been discounted, and upon which the Company is liable, with the Manager or some other official, and endeavour by that means or in any other way he may think advisable, to ascertain what sum will have ultimately to be provided for by the Company. This amount should be carried out as a liability from which there should first be deducted the estimated amount expected to be received from the acceptors.

In the event, however, of the Company becoming insolvent, it would not obtain possession of the Bills, and therefore any amount received from the acceptors would be payable to the holder of the Bills, and not to the Company.

Shareholders' Interest outstanding. When a dividend is declared on the Share Capital it is the usual practice for the Board to draw a cheque on the current account for the full amount, and to place it to the credit of a separate account at the bankers. Interest warrants on the bankers are then issued to the Shareholders for the amount of their respective Shares of the dividend, which on being paid are charged against this separate account.

Owing, perhaps, to the absence of Shareholders from the country, from carelessness, or from other causes, it almost invariably happens that some of these warrants are not presented for a considerable time, and occasionally never come in. In preparing the Balance Sheet the amount of these outstanding interest warrants should be placed among the liabilities under "Outstanding Shareholders' Interest," or some similar heading, while the same amount representing the balance of this separate account at the bankers should be added to the cash balance on the asset side of the Balance Sheet.

Under the heading "Claims admitted, but not paid," which appears in the Balance Sheet of Insurance Companies, should be stated the amounts which have been charged against the Revenue Account for claims under Policies, but not settled at the date of closing the books. Claims admitted but not paid.

The principal item found among the liabilities of a Banking Company is usually the "Amount due on Current and Deposit Accounts," this is the sum of the credit balances of the customers' ledgers, and the Auditor can easily ascertain if the amount is or is not correct. Amount due on Current and Deposit Accounts.

The Auditor should ascertain that a sum has been charged against the Revenue Account, and included among the liabilities in the Balance Sheet, sufficient to provide for any claims likely to arise in respect of contracts entered into by the Company, and in Auditor should require a sufficient Sum to be set apart as a Reserve when Nature of the

Business
requires it.

existence at the date on which the books were closed.

For example, all Companies transacting Insurance business should have a Reserve of this nature for the purpose of meeting claims which it is certain will be made in respect of policies in force at the close of the period under audit.

This sum can, of course, only be an estimate, but it should be calculated on the most reliable data that can be procured, such as the experience of the office in the past, or, if the Company be a new one, that of Companies transacting Insurance business of a similar nature.

For this purpose it may be assumed that the premiums are received, and the claims in respect thereof arise at equal intervals throughout the year, and therefore at the date on which the books are closed, half the risk will have run off the policies then in force.

Mode of
ascertaining
the Reserve
for Insurance
Companies.

The following calculation would then obtain the amount which ought to be charged against the Revenue Account for the year, and included among the liabilities in the Balance Sheet as the Reserve.

(1.) Ascertain from the experience of the Company, or of Companies transacting similar business, the rate per cent. the losses bear to the net premium income.

(2.) Ascertain the amount which bears the same ratio to the net premium income for the year under audit. Half of this amount is the Reserve required.

For
Companies
whose

If the revenue of a Company is derived from annual or other periodical Subscriptions, these are invariably paid in advance, and the privileges Revenue is derived from Subscriptions. acquired thereby are either available from one fixed date to another, or else from the date of the payment of the Subscriptions, according to the regulations of the Company.

In this case the proper Reserve to be charged against the Revenue Account, and included among the liabilities of the Balance Sheet, should, as a rule, consist of the proportions of the Subscriptions applicable to the periods between the date on which the books are closed and those on which the Subscriptions will expire.

For example, supposing an Annual Subscription of four guineas dates from the first of any month, and a Subscriber joins the Company on the 20th October, the Company on closing its books at the 31st December would take credit in its Revenue Account for the four guineas, but against this should be charged on the debit side the three guineas, being the portion of the Subscription applicable to the period between the 1st January and the 30th September of the following year, while the same amount should be brought into the liabilities in the Balance Sheet as a " Reserve to provide for the Liabilities on Current Subscriptions " or a similar heading.

The Auditor must, of course, use his discretion as to whether this precise method of calculating the Reserve should be strictly adhered to in the early years of a Company's existence, but in every case the accurate amount should be ascertained as in the two examples just given, and should form the basis for arriving at the Reserve, and except in the case of a new Company should always be adopted.

Reserve Fund. The " Reserve Fund " of a Company should be the sum representing the excess or part of the excess of the assets over the full liabilities, and the term can only be used honestly with this signification.

As its name implies, the term " Reserve Fund " should be applied solely to the sum set aside and invested to meet an unforeseen or unexpected loss after due provision for all the liabilities has been made. No Balance Sheet can be considered correct which shows on one side a " Reserve Fund," and on the other fictitious assets, such as " Preliminary Expenses," " Balance (deficiency) of the Revenue Account," &c.

Balance of Revenue Account (Surplus). The Surplus brought from the Revenue Account, after allowing for the payment of any dividends or bonus to Shareholders, is usually brought into the debit side of the Balance Sheet. It may, however, be applied towards the reduction of a fictitious Asset Account, or may be added to or form the commencement of a Reserve.

Frequently the Surplus is carried forward from one Revenue Account to the following one; sometimes part only is carried forward and the remainder placed to the credit of the " Reserve."

To this there cannot be any objection. It is always undesirable to have recourse to the " Reserve Fund " for the purpose of paying a dividend or for any other use, and a balance carried from one Revenue Account to the next, or merely placed temporarily to " Reserve," often enables a dividend to be declared without disturbing the Reserve Fund, and consequently avoiding alarm to the Shareholders.

The Assets of a Company may be divided into two *Assets.* classes: Actual and Fictitious.

Among the former class may be enumerated Government Securities, Shares and Debentures in Joint Stock Companies, Freehold and Leasehold Property, Mortgages, Debts due to the Company, Cash, Stock-in-Trade, the amount expended in acquiring or erecting necessary Buildings, Plant, Machinery, &c., while the latter consist of the amounts representing the Expenditure in acquiring the Goodwill of a Business, in the formation of the Company, &c.

Under the general heading of "Government *Government* Securities" may be included all the Investments of *Securities.* the Company the dividends on which are guaranteed by recognised Governments. This heading, however, unless full details are given, is very unsatisfactory, and Companies having miscellaneous investments of this nature may with great advantage adopt the division prescribed by the Life Assurance Companies Act, 1870, Second Schedule, into British, Indian and Colonial, and Foreign Government Securities.

When among the assets of a Company there is *British.* an amount under the heading "British Government Securities," the Auditor should ascertain that only those securities have been included whose dividends are guaranteed by the British Government.

Indian Government and Colonial Government *Indian and* Securities should therefore not be entered here, as the *Colonial.*

dividends thereon are guaranteed only by their respective Governments and not by the Home Government.

It is also desirable, but not necessary, to give the details of each class of security, the amount representing each being stated in an inner column, the total only being extended.

Foreign. The vast difference in the relative value of the securities of Foreign Governments is such that an Auditor should require the name of each investment in Foreign Government Securities with their respective amounts to be set forth.

It would be scarcely more absurd to place before Shareholders a Balance Sheet with the entire property of the Company stated in one amount under the heading " Assets " than to give them one with investments in several Foreign Government Securities under a heading without any details.

While some Governments pay the stipulated interest to the holders of their bonds which are readily saleable, and in some instances are at a premium above their nominal value, others have not paid the interest on their loans for years, and consequently the market value of their Securities are at a considerable discount.

Shares and Debentures in Joint Stock Companies. When a Company holds as an investment the Shares or Debentures of any other Company, the name of each Company, together with the number of the Shares or Debentures held in each, should be stated, also their respective amounts. In the case of Shares the amount paid up on those of each Company should also be stated, and any liability to further calls, but it is not considered a suitable in-

vestment for a Company to hold Shares of other
Companies which are not fully paid up.

If, however, there is any liability attached to
holding Shares in which the money of the Company
is invested, the Shareholders should be made aware
of this fact by its being disclosed in the Balance
Sheet, so that it may either meet with their approval
or cause them to take steps to be released from this
liability by instructing their Directors accordingly.

All Investments should be made in the names of Investments.
should stand
the duly appointed Trustees of the Company, but in the names
of the
should there be none, they should be held in the Trustees.
names of two at least of the Directors and never in
the name of an official of the Company or of one of
the Directors.

It should be distinctly stated whether the values
given to the Investments are the cost price, market
price, or estimated value.

The first named is the most usual one adopted by
Companies, and is certainly the best so long as the
cost price does not exceed the market value. When
an estimated value is inserted the Auditor should
guard against too sanguine a calculation being taken
credit for.

Freehold and Leasehold Property are very fre- Freehold
Property
quently found among the Investments of a Company.
With reference to the former, the Auditor must be
careful that the amount actually paid for the Freehold itself is that which is brought into the assets
as representing its value. All costs and other professional changes incidental to the acquisition of the
Freehold should be charged against the Revenue

Account, and not added to the actual purchase-money.

Leasehold Property. The method of dealing in the accounts with Leasehold Property has been already treated in Chapter VII. The amount which should be brought into the credit side of the Balance Sheet is, of course, the balance of the Ledger Account after the proper amount has been written off and charged against the Revenue Account.

If the Auditor has succeeded another Auditor in his duties, he should of course ascertain if the proper sum has been written off the Lease Accounts and charged against the previous Revenue Accounts, and that the balance as set out among the assets is a fair and proper sum to be there inserted as the present value of the leases.

For this purpose the Table in Appendix B will also be of assistance to him.

Mortgages. Unless the business of the Company, among whose assets the heading " Mortgages " appears, consists solely in making advances abroad, the sums lent on Mortgage on property out of the United Kingdom should be separately stated and not be included under the above general heading without remark.

The Life Assurance Companies Act, 1870, insists on this being done by Life Assurance Companies, and all other Companies should be recommended by their Auditor to follow this example.

Mortgages on freehold and leasehold property should not be mixed up with Mortgages on other property, such as on reversions or life interests, or on stocks or shares. Again, money borrowed on

Mortgage under the authority of an Act of Parliament for a fixed term of years, where the principal is either repaid by equal annual instalments or the principal and interest together in a certain number of years, should not be included under one heading with those Mortgages which can be called in by notice in the usual way.

Unless it is part of the legitimate business of a Company to made advances, the heading " Loans" is a most objectionable one to be found among its assets. *Loans.*

When, however, the funds of a Company have been applied to making advances which have not been repaid at the date of closing the books, the Auditor should ascertain that the amount then due from borrowers has been clearly stated under the above heading. It should not be included among the " Investments " or " Sundry debtors," or disguised under any other heading.

After deducting from the total amount shown in the Company's ledgers to be due to it from its customers, the allowance for bad and doubtful debts charged against the Revenue Account, as explained in Chapter VII, the balance representing the actual amount expected to be ultimately realised should be placed among the assets under " Amounts due from Sundry Debtors," or a similar heading. *Sundry Debtors.*

The amount of the Bills Receivable on Hand may be included under the same heading as the amounts due from sundry debtors, but it is more correct to state it separately. When a Bill Receivable has been discounted, it is, as far as book-keeping is concerned, *Bills Receivable on hand.*

considered equivalent to having been paid, subject to the liability before alluded to, and is not therefore included in the assets.

When a Company employs Agents as a means for obtaining business, the amount either remaining in their hands, or which has to be collected by them and accounted for, should be stated separately among the assets and not included with " Amounts due from Sundry Debtors."

The Auditor should be careful that commission and all other charges which will be allowed to the agents are deducted from their balances and charged against the Revenue Account under their proper headings, so that the difference only, which is the amount the Company should ultimately receive is taken credit for among the assets.

A list of the Agents' Balances should be prepared in the same manner as suggested previously for the sums due from the ordinary debtors, and those amounts which it is considered will not be ultimately realised may be treated as bad or doubtful debts.

When a Company whose Shares are not fully paid up holds any of its own Shares as an investment, the particulars should be clearly set forth in the Balance Sheet and not be included in the amount representing the value of the Shares of other Companies held as an investment.

Unless this be done the Shareholders are not fully aware of the extent of their liability in the event of the Company going into liquidation, for should that happen the Shareholders, in addition to having to meet calls made on their own Shares, would be liable

liable, in the proportion of their respective holdings, to pay the amount which would otherwise be raised by the payment of the calls made on these Shares, were they in the hands of private and responsible owners.

The Interest and Dividends due on Investments, but not received at the date of closing the books, as well as any accrued Interest, should, as stated in Chapter VII, be taken credit for in the Revenue Account, and consequently the same amount must be included among the assets of the Company.

Interest on Investments due and accrued.

Under the heading " Cash at Bankers " may be included not only the balance of a current account, but also any sum that may have been placed on deposit; also any balance in the hands of the Bankers to meet any outstanding Dividend Warrants.

Cash at Bankers.

For the purpose of verifying the correctness of the balance stated in the Balance Sheet to be in the hands of the Company's Bankers, the Auditor should agree it with the Bank Pass Book, and he should take an opportunity of ascertaining at the banking house if the latter be an original document.

The balance shown in the Balance Sheet should be identical with that of the Cash Book, but it is not usual, as previously explained, for this balance to coincide with that found in the Pass Book, for the reason that the latter is affected by cheques *in transitu* both debtor and creditor.

Under the heading " Cash in Hand " should be stated the amount of the balance of the Petty Cash Book not accounted for by any expenditure, and

Cash in hand.

which should, therefore, be in the possession of the Cashier.

As the Auditor seldom commences his duties before at least several days have elapsed after the date on which the books are closed, he can only check the correctness of this balance by ascertaining that the Cashier has in hand the amount unaccounted for by him in the Petty Cash Book at some subsequent date.

Stock-in-Trade.

The amount to be taken credit for among the assets for the Stock-in-Trade is the same as that which appears on the credit side of the Revenue Account.

Office Furniture.

The balance of the Office Furniture Account should be included among the assets, and the Auditor should be satisfied that the amount does not unduly exceed its value.　A percentage should be written off periodically and charged against the Revenue Account for depreciation until the balance of the Ledger Account, representing this asset, has been reduced to the amount representing its value.

Purchase of Business, &c.

When a Company has been formed for the purpose of acquiring and carrying on an established business, the consideration for the acquisition may be either Money, Shares (fully paid up or otherwise), or partly Money and partly Shares.　In any case the consideration can only be entered in the Books of Account as money, under some appropriate heading, such as that in the margin.

So long as the Company is prosperous and its Shareholders receive a satisfactory dividend, this account is apparently as good an asset as a realisable investment, but in the event of the Company going into liquidation the greater part, if not the whole of its value, at once disappears.

It is, therefore, very desirable, instead of dividing all the profits among the Shareholders, for a Sinking Fund to be raised, so that at the end of a certain period this account may be either written off, or reduced in amount to a saleable value. If this plan be adopted also with the fictitious assets accounts, and they have by that means been abolished, the Shareholders will then have their money invested in realisable securities. They will also have, in addition, the goodwill of the business of the Company, and in the event of its failure, they will be able to receive back their Capital in full.

If the Capital of a Company, or even part of it, has been invested in the acquisition of a business for a term of years only, a Sinking Fund should be raised sufficient to redeem the Capital at the expiration of this term.

The foregoing remarks apply to all Companies whose capital or part of it has been expended in the acquisition or establishment of the business, to carry on which it has been formed.

For example: the Capital of a Manufacturing Company is partly required either for acquiring the building, plant, machinery and goodwill of an established business, or in erecting the necessary buildings, purchasing the plant, &c., and creating a market for the sale of its manufactures. That of a Mining Company is partly acquired either for buying a proved and developed mine, with its necessary plant, &c., or

Sinking Fund for same.

in paying wages for sinking the shafts, driving the adits, purchasing bricks, plant &c., and for completing the operations necessary to enable the Company to earn a Revenue in the future.

Plant, &c., purchased under a Hiring Agreement. Plant and Machinery are sometimes purchased under what is known as a Hiring Agreement, that is, an agreement in which it is provided that after the lessee has paid a rent for the use of an article for a certain number of years it shall become his absolute property on the payment of a nominal sum at the expiration of the period. Colliery waggons are frequently purchased under a five years' agreement of this description.

A Company is certainly entitled to take credit among its assets for a proportionate part of any payments of this nature, after charging the Revenue Account with a fair and reasonable amount for usage.

Preliminary Expenses. The expenses incurred incidental to the obtainment of the Share Capital of a Company are usually collected under the heading of "Preliminary Expenses." As it would press unfairly on the Revenue Account of the first year were the total amount thus expended charged against it, it is usual to charge only a proportion, varying from one tenth to one fifth against each year's Revenue Account, and to treat the balance until the Account be thus gradually extinguished as an asset.

The Auditors duty, therefore, in dealing with this account is not to allow any expenses to be included therein but those actually incidental to the obtainment of the Share Capital, or to making the necessary arrangements for the Company to commence its business.

The following disbursements may be properly brought into the " Preliminary Expenses " Account, and any others in addition legitimately and properly expended, as indicated above, connected with the formation and establishment of the Company. *Particulars to be included therein.*

The legal expenses for the preparation of the Memorandum and Articles of Association, the necessary agreements for the purchase of any business or property, filing the necessary documents with the Registrar of Joint Stock Companies, and generally for all the legal work transacted on behalf of the Promoters and Directors of the Company, until the first allotment of Shares has been made, including expenses out of pocket.

The legal and Parliamentary expenses for the obtainment of a private Act of Parliament incorporating the Company, and for obtaining, if necessary, an extension of the same.

The printers' and stationers' bills for printing the Private Act, Parliamentary papers, Memorandum and Articles of Association, prospectuses, notices, plans, books of account, &c.

The advertising account for the advertisement of the prospectus and notices.

The brokerage paid to those employed by the Directors to place the Shares, usually a small percentage on the Capital introduced.

Perhaps the most unsatisfactory item which can be found on the credit side of the Balance Sheet is that representing a deficiency. This is usually the *Balance of Revenue Account (Deficiency).*

result of a loss on the trading brought from the Revenue Account, and as long as it exists no Dividend should be paid to the Shareholders.

The Auditor should require the existence of a deficiency to be clearly set forth in the Balance Sheet, and in such a manner that the amount could not possibly be supposed by the Shareholders to represent an asset.

Balance
Sheet should
be so explicit
as to be
understood
by every
Shareholder.

The Balance Sheet, where finally approved by the Auditor, should be so clearly stated that every Shareholder of ordinary intelligence can understand it. A knowledge of book-keeping is not essential to the comprehension of a Balance Sheet properly drawn. The liabilities and assets should be kept perfectly distinct, each being set forth under their proper headings, and, although according to the recognised method of preparing a Balance Sheet, accounts representing the balance of certain Expenditure Accounts are placed on the same side as the assets, the Auditor should require them to be so stated that they cannot be mistaken for realisable and marketable securities.

CHAPTER IX.

FURTHER REMARKS ON THE DUTIES AND RESPONSIBILITIES OF AUDITORS.

Auditors should be Trained for their Duties—Fallacy of insisting on a Share Qualification—Auditor should be able to suggest Improvements in mode of keeping the Books—An efficient Audit should embrace all the Transactions of the Company—Necessity for providing against bad Debts—Inspection of the Securities—Audit of a Company having Branches—Auditor's Certificate—Position of the Auditor when the Accounts are incorrect—His difficulty in deciding the course to adopt—May be obviated by means of a Special Report—Auditor has many opportunities of suggesting Improvements—Real value of a thorough Audit not yet appreciated by Shareholders—Institute of Chartered Accountants in England and Wales.

It must be evident, after a careful perusal of the foregoing pages, that the duties of an Auditor are not only grave and responsible, as guarding the interests of a number of Shareholders relying on his ability and honesty, but that in order to fulfil them properly he requires, beyond the possession of these necessary qualifications, a perfect knowledge of book-keeping and accounts, also an acquaintance with business matters generally, which can only be possessed by those whose training have been directed to this especial object.

Auditors should be Trained for their Duties.

The absence, however, of these qualifications is strangely not considered an objection by a meeting of Shareholders, when making an election to the important appointment of Auditor of their Company's accounts.

Fallacy of electing a Candidate because he is a Shareholder. One of the most absurd qualifications, and yet the one most frequently put forward by a candidate, is the fact of his being a Shareholder and for this reason alone most incompetent persons are frequently selected to fulfil the office.

Assuming that those thus elected perform their duties with their utmost care and diligence, and to the best of their ability, what will that avail them when they have to deal with statements of Accounts wilfully and fraudulently misrepresented. They are amateurs pitted against professionals, the book-keeper and manager being from the nature of their occupation the latter, while Auditors of the above description must most certainly be classed among amateurs.

To insist on each Director holding a minimum stake in a Company is undoubtedly a wise provision, but to make it a *Sine quâ non* for an Auditor to be a Shareholder is certainly a mistake.

It is true that the possession of an interest in the Company is an incentive to him to look carefully into its accounts, but, as just shown, his ability may not be equal to allowing him to carry out his intentions, and moreover it does not follow that he will use any knowledge gained during his investigation for the benefit of his co-partners.

An Auditor if For example, an Auditor having a very large

interest in a Company whose accounts as presented to him for confirmation, show its affairs to be in a very satisfactory condition, but which on close examination into the Books he finds is not the case, and that the accounts have evidently been prepared with the intention of causing the Shareholders to believe their property to be so far more valuable than it really is, that he knows it is his duty to refuse to certify the accounts, may fail in his duty through selfish motives. *a large Shareholder may fail in his duties through selfish motives.*

He knows that in the event of his refusing to sign the accounts as they are presented to him, and they are consequently altered to show an honest statement of the Company's affairs, the market price of the Shares will fall and his own property be thus depreciated. If, on the other hand, he certifies the accounts as placed before him, the market price of the Shares may be kept up or even rise, and he may then realise his own, with the exception of his qualification. He knows that in the event of the failure of the Company he will not be severely blamed, he will at once plead that he did his best, and that the Shareholders knew he was not a professional Auditor.

An Auditor should be able not only to check and verify the accounts placed before him, but also if he find the Books are kept in a careless manner, or on a bad system, be able to suggest a better method, the adoption of which might not only save expense but also ensure greater accuracy in recording the transactions of the Company. *Auditor should be able to suggest Improvements in Book-keeping if necessary.*

The offices of many Companies are overburdened

with unnecessary detail, a large number of subsidiary books being employed which might be concentrated in a fewer number, or perhaps even be dispensed with altogether.

An efficient Audit should embrace the Examination of all Transactions. A thorough and efficient Audit should embrace an examination of all the transactions of a Company, and an Auditor acting on this principle would ascertain that all had been duly entered and discharged. A purchase made, a sale effected, or any matter of business transacted, and once entered in one of the subsidiary Books, becomes part of a system, with which it is so incorporated that it cannot be omitted, overlooked, or cancelled, without so disarranging the organisation, that an efficient Auditor would at once detect either the carelessness or the fraud.

A careful note should be taken by the Auditor of the age of the balances at the debit of the personal accounts in the ledgers, and he should inquire the reason why those of more than say six months' standing have not been either settled or reduced in amount.

Necessity for Providing for bad Debts. It is very important that due provision be made periodically for bad and doubtful debts, otherwise there will appear among the assets in successive Balance Sheets an increasing amount due from the debtors of the Company which will ultimately attract the attention of the Shareholders. On inquiry being made and the true value of these outstanding accounts ascertained, it may be found on writing down this asset to its value that the difference absorbs part or the whole of the net profits taken credit for in the period under audit, and consequently no Dividend can be declared.

Nothing is more distasteful to Shareholders than to find, after regularly receiving good Dividends, they must be either reduced in amount or discontinued, because, not having been legitimately earned, they have been paid to them out of their own Capital.

This is, however, continually occurring, sometimes through the discovery of amounts having been added to the Capital Accounts which ought to have been charged against Revenue, sometimes, through due provision not having been made for bad and doubtful debts, and frequently through a sufficient amount not having been periodically charged against the Revenue Account for depreciation in the value of plant, machinery, stock-in-trade, &c., or for the exhaustion of a lease.

Having completed his investigation of the Accounts, and being satisfied as to their correctness, so far as figures are concerned, the Auditor should then inspect the Securities representing the assets, and ascertain that they are in the possession of the Company free, and unencumbered by mortgages, or any charges, unless the fact of their being so charged is clearly stated in the accounts. *Inspection of the Securities.*

In order that this may be done in a business-like and methodical manner, the Auditor should have prepared for him a list of the Securities, arranged under the headings in which they appear in the Balance Sheet. The full particulars of each Security should be given, with its value as taken credit for in that document.

The Auditor must be careful that the Securities deposited by those to whom the Company has made advances are accompanied by the necessary bonds, undertaking to repay either on demand, or on the expiration of a stipulated period, the sums advanced, with the interest thereon, also undertaking to deposit fresh Securities with the Company in the event of the market price of those in its possession being unduly depreciated during the continuance of the loan. He should also see that the coupons are attached to all certificates payable to bearer.

Audit of a Company having Branches. When a Company has Branches in the country or abroad it is, of course, impossible for the Auditor to make such a thorough investigation of its affairs as it is his duty to do when all the records of the business are kept in one office. The principal books are open to his inspection, and he should critically examine the returns from the Branches, and ascertain they are properly amalgamated with the books kept at the head office.

It is very important that, where another person's figures are taken as correct, the Auditor should require him to give a Certificate of their correctness, and he should only sign the Accounts which are to be laid before the Shareholders subject to such certificate. It is then, of course, at the discretion of the Shareholders whether they shall be content with this partial audit, or whether they shall instruct their Auditor to visit all or some of the Branches for the purpose of verifying the correctness of the returns.

Auditor's Certificate. On the completion of his investigation, it is usual for the Auditor to append a Certificate to the Accounts, that they are either correct or that, in his opinion, they do not represent accurately the transactions and position of the Company.

There is no form of Certificate prescribed by any of the Public Acts, and it is usually left to the Auditor as to how he shall convey to the Shareholders his opinion of the Accounts he has audited.

One of the most unpleasant situations in which an Auditor can be placed is when he feels that he cannot append his Certificate to the Accounts he has audited without qualification. *Position of the Auditor when the Accounts are incorrect.*

Of course, in those cases where they are grossly inaccurate, whether prepared unintentionally or for the purpose of misleading the Shareholders or the customers of the Company, or with the view to inducing the public to take up additional Shares, then the duty of the Auditor is clear.

He must positively refuse to give his unqaulified Certificate, but at the same time may intimate his willingness to do so provided the Accounts be redrawn so as to present an honest and correct statement of the transactions and position of the Company.

It frequently happens that Directors, owing perhaps to depression in trade, which they have reason to believe is only temporary, will, without any intention of acting dishonorably, present a Revenue Account showing a profit equal to that of preceding years, while in fact it is considerably less.

To any one not versed in Accounts this may appear impossible, but it is undoubtedly of very frequent occurrence.

When a Company is prosperous, an Auditor has

usually very little trouble in arranging for a proper allowance for depreciation of stock-in-trade, plant, machinery, &c., to be charged against the Revenue Account, but when a period of depression in trade arises, there is frequently great difficulty in persuading the Directors to continue this wholesome practice. A variety of excuses are made for its discontinuance, and if the Auditor receives an actual refusal to amend the Accounts, it is not always easy to resolve on what course to pursue.

His difficulty in deciding what course to adopt. It may be argued, that as each Shareholder is a partner in the undertaking, they should be informed by their Auditor that the profits of the period referred to are not calculated on the same strict basis as hitherto, but the fact must not be overlooked that this information may be so made use of by a single Shareholder as to depreciate or even totally destroy the future of the Company.

To refuse to sign the Accounts, or to insert in his Certificate that they are incorrect, might therefore be followed by results very disastrous to the Company, and consequently to the Shareholders whose representative the Auditor is.

May be obviated by means of a Special Report to the Members. The best plan an Auditor can adopt under these circumstances is to address to the Members a full Report on the Accounts, setting forth clearly therein the points at issue between the Directors and himself, and then sign the Accounts as Auditor in the usual manner subject to this Report.

This Auditor's Report should be forwarded to the Shareholders of the Company with the Accounts. They will then have the opportunity of considering what steps they shall take at the meeting, and on being brought together will decide whether to adopt the Accounts as presented by the Directors, or to reject them and pass a resolution that they be amended as recommended by their Auditor in his Report.

The Auditor must, of course, use his discretion as to the necessity of issuing a Special Report of this nature. As long as the assets are not overestimated in the Accounts he has not any right to insist on the Directors continuing a practice of charging the Revenue Account with allowances for depreciation, which, perhaps, although not always necessary, they had no objection to do out of large profits. Should, however, he feel sure the assets have really depreciated in value since the last Balance Sheet was taken out, then it is clearly his duty to acquaint the Shareholders with this fact should it not be disclosed in the Accounts.

It is not sufficient for the Auditor to merely forward this Report to the Board of Directors, he must be satisfied that either a copy or an intimation of its existence has been forwarded to every Shareholder with the Accounts. *Which the Auditor must be satisfied reaches the Members.*

Should he ascertain the Directors have suppressed his Report, he should intimate by letter or circular to every Shareholder the fact of its existence, and not until this has been done are his obligations to the Shareholders discharged.

Fortunately, however, it is not often an Auditor comes into conflict with the Directors in this manner. Both they and he have, as a rule, the *Auditor has many opportunities of suggesting Improve-*

ments in Administration.

same interests at heart, namely, the prosperity and welfare of the Company, and in his capacity as an ally and assistant of the Directors in all matters concerning the welfare of the Shareholders, an Auditor has many opportunities of pointing out to them various improvements which might with advantage be adopted, not only in the book-keeping department, but also in the general routine work of the office.

As already stated, in many Companies, more especially in large ones, the amount of detail passed and repassed through the books is wholly unnecessary, and an efficient Auditor has many opportunities of suggesting alterations, which would, if adopted, greatly lessen labour, and consequently expense.

But has not any right to insist on their being adopted.

It is very important that in his anxiety to do his duty towards the Shareholders the Auditor should be careful not to interfere in the management of the Company by insisting on the adoption of any of his propositions as to the system of book-keeping, the interior economy of the office, or in any other matter. He should endeavour to introduce his reforms by friendly suggestions, and by putting them forward gradually.

Directors are Managers of the Company.

The Directors are the Managers of the Company on behalf of the Shareholders, to whom they are alone responsible, and the strict duty of the Auditor is to ascertain that the Accounts as presented to the latter show accurately the result of this management. It is by performing this duty conscientiously and efficiently he can best discharge his obligation to those who have elected him to his responsible position.

The real value of a thorough and systematic Audit of the Accounts of Public Companies is not, however, at present adequately appreciated by Shareholders, but the very severe lessons the investing public have learnt through the failures of the last few years is certainly causing them to pay more attention to the qualifications of those who undertake the duties of Auditors.

Real value of a thorough Audit not yet appreciated.

This fact is so well recognised by promoters that nearly all the prospectuses of new Companies now include among their officers the names of professional Accountants as their Auditors, while the older Companies are gradually replacing the Shareholders' Auditor by a professional one.

On the 11th May, 1880, a Royal Charter was granted by Her Majesty's Privy Council incorporating the London Institute of Accountants and other Accountants' Societies into one Institute, under the style of "The Institute of Chartered Accountants in England and Wales," membership of which can only be obtained by duly qualified Accountants.

Institute of Chartered Accountants in England and Wales.

There is now, therefore, a recognised body of professional Auditors known as Chartered Accountants, who are, of course, amenable to the Institute for the proper fulfilment of their duties.

To explain the nature of these duties, and to show that it requires both training and experience in order to perform them efficiently, has been the endeavour of the author, and in conclusion he expresses the hope that the work will be found useful by members of the Institute, as well as by others on whom has been conferred by Shareholders the important and responsible appointments of Auditors of their Companies' Accounts.

APPENDIX A.

BALANCE SHEET PRESCRIBED BY COMPANIES ACT, 1862. TABLE A.

FORM OF ACCOUNTS PRESCRIBED BY REGULATION OF RAILWAYS ACT, 1868.

FORM OF ANNUAL ACCOUNTS PRESCRIBED BY GASWORKS CLAUSES ACT (1847) AMENDMENT.

FORM OF ANNUAL ACCOUNTS PRESCRIBED BY LIFE ASSURANCE COMPANIES ACT, 1870.

ANNUAL RETURN AS PRESCRIBED BY THE CHIEF REGISTRAR UNDER THE FRIENDLY SOCIETIES ACT, 1875. FORMS A AND B.

RECEIPTS AND EXPENDITURE ACCOUNT (PRO FORMÂ).

REVENUE ACCOUNT (PRO FORMÂ).

BALANCE SHEET (PRO FORMÂ).

*Balance Sheet prescribed by Companies Act, 1862.—*TABLE A.

Dr.   BALANCE SHEET of the   Co. made up to   18   Cr.

CAPITAL AND LIABILITIES.

I. CAPITAL

Showing:
1. The Number of Shares
2. The Amount paid per Share
3. If any arrears of Calls, the Nature of the Arrear, and the Names of the Defaulters.
4. The Particulars of any forfeited Shares.

II. DEBTS AND LIABILITIES of the Company.

Showing:
5. The Amount of Loans on Mortgages or Debenture Bonds.
6. The Amount of Debts owing by the Company, distinguishing—
   - (a.) Debts for which Acceptances have been given.
   - (b.) Debts to Tradesmen for Supplies of Stock in Trade or other Articles.
   - (c.) Debts for Law Expenses.
   - (d.) Debts for Interest on Debentures or other Loans.
   - (e.) Unclaimed Dividends.
   - (f.) Debts not enumerated above.

VI. RESERVE FUND.

Showing:
The Amount set aside from Profits to meet Contingencies.

VII. PROFIT AND LOSS.

Showing:
The Disposable Balance for Payment of Dividend, &c.

CONTINGENT LIABILITIES.

Claims against the Company not acknowledged as Debts.
Moneys for which the Company is contingently liable.

PROPERTY AND ASSETS.

III. PROPERTY held by the Company.

Showing:
7. Immovable Property, distinguishing—
   - (a.) Freehold Land
   - (b.)   ,,   Buildings
   - (c.) Leasehold ,,
8. Movable Property, distinguishing—
   - (d.) Stock in Trade
   - (e.) Plant

The Cost to be stated with Deductions for Deterioration in Value as charged to the Reserve Fund or Profit and Loss.

IV. DEBTS owing to the Company.

Showing:
9. Debts considered good, for which the Company hold Bills or other Securities.
10. Debts considered good for which the Company hold no Security.

Debts considered doubtful and bad.

11. Any Debt due from a Director or other Officer of the Company to be separately stated.

V. CASH AND INVESTMENTS.

Showing:
12. The Nature of Investment and Rate of Interest.
13. The Amount of Cash, where lodged, and if bearing Interest.

Forms of Account prescribed by Regulation of Railways Act, 1868.

RAILWAY.   Half Year ending   18

[No. 1.]   STATEMENT OF CAPITAL AUTHORISED, AND CREATED BY
THE COMPANY.

ACTS OF PARLIAMENT, or Certificates of the Board of Trade.	CAPITAL AUTHORIZED.			CAPITAL CREATED OR SANCTIONED.			BALANCE.		
	Stock and Shares.	Loans.	Total.	Stock and Shares.	Loans.	Total.	Stock and Shares.	Loans.	Total.
1. ⎤	£	£	£	£	£	£	£	£	£
2. ⎟ [Except where Capital Powers are comprised									
3. ⎟ in a Consolidation Act, each Act or Certificate									
4. ⎟ authorizing Capital to be stated here sepa-									
5. ⎟ rately in order of Date.]									
&c. ⎦									
TOTAL									

[No. 2.]   STATEMENT OF STOCK AND SHARE CAPITAL CREATED, SHOWING
THE PROPORTION RECEIVED.

DESCRIPTION.	Amount created.	Amount received.	Calls in arrear.	Amount uncalled.	Amount unissued.
[State each Class of Stock or Shares in order of Date of Creation, showing the Premium or Discount, if any, at which it was issued, the Preferential or fixed Dividends, if any, to which it is entitled, and any other Conditions attached to it.]	£	£	£	£	£
TOTAL					

[No. 3.] CAPITAL RAISED BY LOANS AND DEBENTURE STOCK.

	RAISED BY LOANS.									RAISED BY ISSUE OF DEBENTURE STOCKS.			Total raised by Loans and by Debenture Stocks.
—	At per Cent.	At per Cent.	At per Cent.	At per Cent.	At per Cent.	At per Cent.	At per Cent.	At per Cent.	Total Loans.	At per Cent.	At per Cent.	Total Debenture Stocks.	
	£	£	£	£	£	£	£	£	£	£	£	£	£ s. d.
Existing at Ditto at													
Increase ... Decrease ...													

Total Amount authorised to be raised by Loans and by Debenture Stocks in respect of Capital created, as per Statement No. 1 ...
Total Amount raised by Loans and by Debenture Stock, as above...

Balance being available Borrowing Powers at   186

[No. 4.] RECEIPTS AND EXPENDITURE ON CAPITAL ACCOUNT.

Dr.   *Cr.*

	Amount Expended to	Amount Expended during Half Year.	Total.		Amount Received to	Amount Received during Half Year.	Total.
	£ s. d.	£ s. d.	£ s. d.		£ s. d.	£ s. d.	£ s. d.
To Expenditure— On Lines open for Traffic (No. 5)... On Lines in course of Construction (No. 5) ... ... Working Stock (No. 5) ... ... Subscriptions to other Railways (No. 5) ... ... Docks, Steamboats, and other special Items (No. 5) ...				By Receipts— Shares and Stock, per Account No. 2 ... ... Loans, per Account No. 3 ... ... Debenture Stock, per Account No. 3 ... ... Sundries (in detail)...			
„ Balance							

[No. 5.]　DETAILS OF CAPITAL EXPENDITURE, for Half Year ending　18

Lines open for Traffic— 　Particulars— Lines in course of Con- 　struction— 　Particulars—	[Showing under separate Heads, Amount paid 　for Land (Purchase and Compensation), 　Construction of Way and Stations, includ- 　ing Rails, Chairs, Sleepers, &c., Engineering 　and Surveying, Law Charges, Parliamentary 　Expenses, Interest, Commission, &c.]

Working Stock—
　Particulars—Showing each Description of Stock　...　...
Subscriptions to other Railways—
　Particulars—Stating Lines　...　...　...　...
Docks, Steamboats, and other special Items—
　Particulars　...　...　...　...　...　...

　　　Total Expenditure for Half Year, as per Account No. 4　...

[No. 6.]　　　RETURN OF WORKING STOCK.

	LOCOMO-TIVE.		COACHING.					MERCHANDISE AND MINERAL.							
	Engines.	Tenders.	First Class.	Second Class.	Third Class.			Goods Waggons.	Goods Waggons covered.	Coke Trucks.	Cattle Trucks.	Timber Trucks.				
Stock on the　18																
Ditto on the　18																
Increase during the Half Year　...																
Decrease during the Half Year　...																

[No. 7.]　ESTIMATE OF FURTHER EXPENDITURE ON CAPITAL ACCOUNT.

	FURTHER EXPENDITURE.		
	During the Half Year ending	In subse-quent Half Years.	Total.
Lines open for Traffic　...　...　...　... 　(Particulars showing principal Items.)			
Lines in course of Construction　...　...　... 　(Details of each Line.)			
Working Stock　...　...　...　... 　(Particulars.)			
Subscription to other Railways　...　...　... 　(Specifying Lines.)			
Docks, Steamboats, and other Special Items　... 　(Particulars.)			
Works not yet commenced and in abeyance (in detail)			
Other Items (in detail)　...　...　...　...			
Total estimated further Expenditure of Capital ...			

[No. 8.]　CAPITAL POWERS AND OTHER ASSETS AVAILABLE TO MEET
　　　　FURTHER EXPENDITURE, as per No. 7.

Share and Loan Capital authorised or created but not yet received
Any other Assets (in detail) ...　...　...　...　...
　　　　Total　...　...　...　...　...

[No. 9] *Dr.*   REVENUE ACCOUNT.   *Cr.*

Half Year ended	EXPENDITURE.	£ s. d.	Half Year ended	RECEIPTS.	£ s. d.	£ s. d.
	To Maintenance of Way, Works, and Stations... } See Abstract A.			By Passengers............		
				„ Parcels, Horses, Carriages, &c............		
	„ Locomotive Power...do. B.			„ Mails		
	„ Carriage and Waggon Repairs ...... } do. C.					
	„ Traffic Expenses......do. D.			„ Merchandise		
	„ General Charges......do. E.			„ Live Stock............		
	„ Law Charges			„ Minerals..............		
	„ Parliamentary Expenses...					
	„ Compensation (Accidents and Losses)			„ Special and Miscellaneous Receipts— *Such as Navigations, Steamboats, Rents, Transfer Fees, &c.*		
	„ Rates and Taxes					
	„ Government Duty					
	„ Special and Miscellaneous Expenses (if any)			*Details.*		
	„ Balance carried to Net Revenue Account					
	£			£		

[No. 10.] *Dr.*   NET REVENUE ACCOUNT.   *Cr.*

Half Year ended		£ s. d.	Half Year ended		£ s. d.
	To Interest on Mortgage and Debenture Loans			By Balance brought from last Half Year's Account	
	„ Interest on Debenture Stock				
	„ Interest on Calls in Advance			„ Ditto, Revenue Account, No. 9 ......,...............	
	„ Interest on Temporary Loans				
	„ Interest on Lloyd's Bonds .				
	„ Interest on Banking Balances			„ Dividends on Shares in other Companies	
	„ General Interest Account (if in Debit)				
	„ Rents of Leased Lines, Guarantees, &c.			„ Bankers and General Interest Account (if in Credit)	
	Details				
	„ Special and Miscellaneous Payments (if any)			„ Special and Miscellaneous Receipts (if any)	
	Details.				
	„ Balance, being Payment available for Dividend ...			(*Detail to be given.*)	
	[*See No.* 13.] £			£	

[No. 11.] PROPOSED APPROPRIATION OF BALANCE AVAILABLE FOR DIVIDENDS.

Half Year ended	
	Balance available for Dividend as per Account No. 10............£
	Preference Stock } to be stated in order of Creation, { £
	Ditto with Rate of Dividend.
	Ditto
	Ordinary Stock (being at the Rate of per cent.)......
	Balance to next Half Year......... £

[No. 12.]   ABSTRACTS.

A. MAINTENANCE OF WAY, WORKS, &c.		
Half Year ended	£ s. d.	£ s. d.
Salaries, Office Expenses, and General Superintendence		
Maintenance and Renewal of Permanent Way		
Wages..............		
Materials...........		
Repairs of Roads, Bridges, Signals, and Works		
Repairs of Stations and Buildings		
Special Expenditure (if any)		
MILES MAINTAINED :		
Double		
Single		
Total		
Total......		

B. LOCOMOTIVE POWER.		
Half Year ended	£ s. d.	£ s. d.
Salaries, Office Expenses, and General Superintendence		
RUNNING EXPENSES :		
Wages connected with the working of Locomotive Engines		
Coal and Coke		
Water		
Oil, Tallow, and other Stores		
REPAIRS & RENEWALS :		
Wages................		
Materials..............		
Special Expenditure ...		
£		

C. REPAIRS AND RENEWALS OF CARRIAGES AND WAGGONS.		
Half Year ended	£ s. d.	£ s. d.
CARRIAGES :		
Salaries, Office Expenses, and General Superintendence ...		
Wages..................		
Materials..............		
WAGGONS :		
Salaries, Office Expenses, and General Superintendence ...		
Wages..................		
Materials..............		
Total........		

D. TRAFFIC EXPENSES.	
Half Year ended	£ s. d.
Salaries and Wages, &c.	
Fuel, Lighting, Water, and General Stores	
Clothing...........................	
Printing, Stationery, and Tickets	
Horses, Harness, Vans, Provender, &c.....................	
Waggon Covers, Ropes, &c....	
Joint Station Expenses	
Miscellaneous Expenses	
Special Expenditure (if any) .	

E. GENERAL CHARGES.	
Half Year ended	£ s. d.
Directors	
Auditors and Public Accountants (if any)	
Salaries of Secretary, General Manager, Accountant, and Clerks........................	
Office Expenses ditto ditto	
Advertising	
Fire Insurance	
Electric Telegraph Expenses .	
Railway Clearing House Expenses............................	
Special Expenditure (if any) .	

[No. 13.] *Dr.*   GENERAL BALANCE SHEET.   *Cr.*

To Capital Account, Balance at Credit thereof, as per Account No. 4.......................	£	s.	d.	By Cash at Bankers — Current Account	£	s.	d.
„ Net Revenue Account, Balance at Credit thereof, as per Account No. 10				„ Cash on Deposit at Interest .			
„ Unpaid Dividends and Interest				„ Cash invested in Consols and Government Securities			
„ Guaranteed Dividends and Interest payable or accruing and provided for				„ Cash invested in Shares of other Railway Companies not charged as Capital Expenditure			
„ Temporary Loans................				„ General Stores — Stock of Materials on hand............			
„ Lloyd's Bonds and other Obligations not included in Loan Capital Statement, No. 3 ...				„ Traffic Accounts due to the Company			
„ Balance due to Bankers				„ Amounts due by other Companies			
„ Debts due to other Companies				„ Do. Clearing House			
„ Amount due to Clearing House				„ Do. Post Office			
„ Sundry Outstanding Accounts				„ Sundry Outstanding Accounts			
„ Fire Insurance Fund on Stations, Works, and Buildings				„ Suspense Accounts (if any)... *To be enumerated.*			
„ Insurance Fund on Steamboats				„ Special Items			
„ Special Items							
	£				£		

[No. 14.]   MILEAGE STATEMENT.

Half Year ended		Miles authorised.	Miles constructed.	Miles constructing or to be constructed.	Miles worked by Engines.
	Lines owned by Company				
	Do. partly owned				
	Do. leased or rented...............				
	Total.........				
	Do. worked				
	Foreign Lines worked over				
	Total.........				

[No. 15.]   STATEMENT OF TRAIN MILEAGE.

Half Year ended.		
	Passenger Trains	
	Goods and Mineral Trains	
	Total.....................	

(Signed)   *Chairman or Deputy Chairman of Company.*
                            Secretary or Accountant of Company.

CERTIFICATE RESPECTING THE PERMANENT WAY, &c.

I hereby certify that the whole of the Company's Permanent Way, Stations, Buildings, Canals, and other Works have during the past Half Year been maintained in good Working Condition and Repair.

Date   18   *Engineer.*

CERTIFICATE RESPECTING THE ROLLING STOCK.

I hereby certify that the whole of the Company's Plant, Engines, Tenders, Carriages, Waggons, Machinery, and Tools, also the Marine Engines of the Steam Vessels, have during the past Half Year been maintained in good Working Order and Repair.   { *Chief Engineer, or*
Date   18 .   { *Locomotive Superintendent.*

AUDITOR'S CERTIFICATE.

As prescribed by Act 30 and 31 Victoria, Cap. 127, to follow.

Forms of Accounts prescribed by Gasworks Clauses Act (1847) Amendment.

The   GAS COMPANY.—Year ended 31st December, 18 .

A.—STATEMENT OF SHARE CAPITAL on the 31st December, 18 .

1 Description of Capital.	2 Maximum Dividend authorised	3 Number of Shares issued.	4 Nominal Amount of Share.	5 Called up per Share.	6 Total paid up.	7 Amount issued but not paid up.	8 Remaining to be issued.	9 Total Amounts authorised

B.—STATEMENT OF LOAN CAPITAL, on the 31st December, 18 .

1 Description of Loan (Mortgage, Bond, Debenture, Stock, &c.).	2 Rate per Cent. of Interest.	3 Total Amounts borrowed at 31st December, 18 .	4 Remaining to be borrowed.	5 Total Amounts authorised.

Total Share Capital paid up (see A) .... £
Do.   Loan   do.   borrowed (see B) .... £

Total Capital received...... £

C.—CAPITAL ACCOUNT, for the Year ended 31st December, 18 .

	Expenditure to 31st Dec., 18 .	Expended this Year.	Total to 31st Dec., 18 .		Certified Receipts 31st Dec., 18 .	Received during Year.	Total Receipts to 31st Dec., 18 .
	£ s. d.	£ s. d.	£ s. d.		£ s. d.	£ s. d.	£ s. d.
1. To Expenditure to 31st December, 18 *Since that date.*				1. By Ordinary Shares of £ each			
2. To Lands acquired, including Law Charges				2. By ditto of £ each			
3. To new Buildings, Manufacturing Plant, Machines, Storage Works, and other Structures connected with Manufacture ...				3. By Preference Shares of £ each			
				4. By Debenture Stock			
4. To new Mains and Service Pipes (not being in place of old ones) including laying same, Paving, and other works connected with distribution ...				5. By Mortgages and Bonds			
				6. By Amount received in anticipation of Calls			
5. To new Metres (not in place of old ones), including fixing							
6. To Costs of promoting Special Act							
7. To Special Items (if any)...................							
Total Expenditure .... To Balance of Capital Account		£			Total..................		

D.—Revenue Account, for the Year ended 31st December, 18

	£ s. d.	£ s. d.		£ s. d.	£ s. d.
To Manufacture of Gas.			**By Sale of Gas.**		
1. Coals, including Dues, Carriage, Unloading, and all Expenses of depositing same on Works			1. Common Gas (cubic feet), at / per 1000 cubic feet		
2. Purifying Materials, Oil, Water, and Sundries at Works			2. Cannel Gas (cubic feet), at / per 1000 cubic feet		
3. Salaries of Engineers, including Chief Engineer (if any), Superintendents, and Officers at Works			3. Public Lighting and Under Contracts		
4. Wages and Gratuities at Works			4. Rental of Meters		
5. Repairs and Maintenance of Works and Plant (including renewal of Retorts), Machines, Apparatus, Tools, Materials, and Labour ....£			**By Residual Products.**		
Less Old Material sold ......£			5. Coke, less Labour and Cartage		
To Distribution of Gas.			6. Breeze, ditto		
6. Salaries of Surveyor, Chief Inspector, Inspectors, Assistant Inspectors, and Clerks in Light Office			7. Tar, ditto		
7. Repair, Maintenance, and Renewal of Mains, and of Service Pipes, including Materials, Laying and Paving, and Labour			8. Ammoniacal Liquor, ditto.........		
8. Repairing, Renewing, and Refixing Meters			9. By Rents............		
To Public Lamps.			10. By Transfer Fees		
9. Lighting and Repairing			By other Items (if any)		
To Rents, Rates, and Taxes.					
10. Rents					
11. Rates and Taxes.................					
To Management.					
12. Directors' Allowances					
13. Salaries of Secretary, Accountant and Clerks, Office Keepers, and Messengers ...					
14. Collectors' Commission or Salaries					
15. Stationery and Printing					
16. General Establishment Charges and Incidentals					
17. Auditor					
To Law and Parliamentary Charges.					
18. Law...............................					
19. Parliamentary (oppositions)...					
20. To Depreciation Fund for Works on Leasehold Lands (if any)					
21. To Bad Debts....................					
To other Items (if any)					
Total Expenditure..............					
Balance carried to Profit and Loss Account, E			Total Receipts..		

E.—Profit and Loss Account (Net Revenue), for the Year ended 31st December, 18

Dr.   *Cr.*

	£ s. d.		£ s. d.
1. To amount carried to Reserved Fund Account, F (if any), from Profits of 18		1. By Balance of Net Profit brought from last Account (31st December, 18)...............	
2. „ Interest on Temporary Loans, and Moneys received in anticipation of Calls ...		2. „ Amount drawn from Reserved Fund (if any)	
3. „ Ditto on Mortgages and Bonds accrued to 31st December, 18		Less Dividend paid for the Half Year ended 31st December, 18 .	
4. „ Ditto on Debenture Stock to ditto		3. Balance brought from Revenue Account, D, being Profit for Year to December, 18	
5. „ Half-year's Dividend on 1st Preferential to 30th June, 18		4. Interest on Moneys deposited	
6. „ Ditto, 2nd Preferential to ditto			
7. „ Ditto on Ordinary Shares at per Cent.			
„ Balance of Net Profit to be carried to next Account, subject to Half-year's Dividends to 31st December, 18			
£		£	

F.—Reserved Fund Account, for the Year ended 31st December, 18 .

	£ s. d.		£ s. d.
1. Amount (if any) carried to Profit and Loss Account, E, to make up deficiencies of Dividends to 31st December, 18		1. By Balance brought from last Account	
2. Amount Paid for Extraordinary Claim or Demand (if any)............................		2. „ Balance brought from Profit and Loss Account, (E)	
3. Amount of Balance to be carried to next Account.........		3. „ Interest on Amount Invested	
£		£	

Like Accounts must be given for Depreciation Fund for Works on Leaseholds (if any).

G.—Statement of Coals, during the Year ended 31st December, 18

Description of Coal.	In Store, 31st December, 18	Received during Year.	Carbonized or used during Year.	In Store, 31st December, 18
	Tons.	Tons.	Tons.	Tons.
Common				
Cannel				

H.—STATEMENT OF RESIDUAL PRODUCTS, for the Year ended 31st December, 18 .

Description of Residual.	In Store, 31st December, 18 . Estimated.	Made during Year. Estimated	Used in Manufacture during Year. Estimated.	Sold during Year.	In Store, 31st December, 18 Estimated.
Coke, Common, chaldrons of 36 bushels					
Cannel ,, ,,					
Breeze ,, ,,					
Tar, gallons					
Ammoniacal Liquor, butts of 108 gallons					

I.—GENERAL BALANCE SHEET, on 31st December, 18 .

Dr.   *Cr.*

	£ s. d.		£ s. d.
1. *To Capital Account—* Balance at Credit thereof (Account C)		1. By Cash at Bankers......	
2. ,, *Profit and Loss Account—* Balance at Credit thereof (Account E)		2. ,, Cash on Deposit or at Interest	
3. ,, *Reserved Fund—* Balance at Credit thereof (Account F)		3. ,, Coals for Stock on hand, 31st December, 18	
4. ,, *Depreciation Fund* (for Works on Leasehold Lands)— Balance at Credit thereof (Account)............		4. ,, Coke and Breeze, 31st December, 18	
5. ,, Unpaid Dividends		5. ,, Tar and other Products, 31st December, 18	
6. ,, Interest accrued and unpaid on Mortgages, Bonds, and Debenture Stock, and other Loans, to 31st December, 18		6. ,, Sundry Stores, 31st December, 18 ..,	
		7. ,, Gas and Meter Rental; Balance of this Account due to the Company on 31st December, 18 , less Deposits and Prepayments	
7. ,, Sundry Tradesmen and others, for Amount due for Coals, Stores, &c., to 31st December, 18		8. ,, Coke and other Residual, 31st December, 18	
8. ,, *Wages and Contingencies—* Amount due to 31st December, 18		9. ,, SundryAccounts, 31st December, 18 ...	
,, Other Items (if any)		,, Special Items (if any), including Investments ...	
£		£	

FORM OF ANNUAL ACCOUNTS PRESCRIBED BY LIFE ASSURANCE COMPANIES ACT, 1870.

FIRST SCHEDULE.

REVENUE ACCOUNT of the   for the Year ending

18 (Date)		£ s. d.	18 (Date)		£ s. d
	Amount of Funds at the beginning of the Year...			Claims under Policies (after deduction of Sums Re-assured)....................	
	Premiums			Surrenders	
	Consideration for Annuities granted			Annuities	
	Interest and Dividends ...			Commission	
	Other Receipts (Accounts to be specified)...........			Expenses of Management .	
				Dividends and Bonuses to Shareholders (if any) ...	
				Other Payments (Accounts to be specified)...........	
				Amount of Funds at the end of the Year, as per second Schedule	
	£			£	

Note 1.—Companies having separate accounts for Annuities to return the particulars of their Annuity business in a separate statement.

Note 2.—Items in this and in the accounts in the Third and Fifth Schedules should be the net amounts after deduction of the amounts paid and received in respect of Re-assurances.

SECOND SCHEDULE.

BALANCE SHEET of the   on the   18

LIABILITIES.	£ s. d.	ASSETS.	£ s. d.
Shareholders' Capital paid up (if any) ....£		Mortgages on Property within the United Kingdom	
Assurance Fund...............		Mortgages on Property out of the United Kingdom............	
Annuity Fund (if any)		Loans on the Company's Policies	
Other Funds (if any) to be specified		Investments—	
		In British Government Securities	
Total Funds, as per First Schedule.........................		Indian and Colonial Government Securities	
Claims admitted but not paid*...		Foreign Government Securities	
Other Sums owing by the Company* (Accounts to be specified)..............................		Railway and other Debentures and Debenture Stocks	
		Railway Shares (Preference and Ordinary)...............	
		House Property	
		Other Investments (to be specified).....................	
		Loans upon Personal Security...	
		Agents' Balances	
		Outstanding Premiums...........	
		Do. Interest	
		Cash—On Deposit ....£ In Hand and on Current Account	
		Other Assets (to be specified) ...	
£		£	

* *Note.*—These items are included in the corresponding items in the First Schedule.

THIRD SCHEDULE.

REVENUE ACCOUNTS of the   for the Year ending

No. 1.—LIFE ASSURANCE ACCOUNT.

(Date)		£ s. d.	(Date)		£ s. d.
	Amount of Life Assurance Fund at the beginning of the year..................			Claims under Life Policies (after deduction of sums Re-assured)	
	Premiums, after deduction of Re-assurance Premiums			Surrenders	
				Annuities	
	Consideration for Annuities granted			Commission	
	Interest and Dividends ...			Expenses of Management .	
	Other Receipts (accounts to be specified)...........			Other Payments (accounts to be specified)...........	
				Amount of Life Assurance Fund at the end of the year, as per Fourth Schedule	
	£			£	

Note.—Companies having separate accounts for Annuities to return the particulars of their Annuity business in a separate statement.

No. 2.—FIRE ACCOUNT.

Amount of Fire Insurance Fund at the beginning of the year		Losses by Fire (after deduction of Re-assurances)...	
Premiums received, after deduction of Re-assurances		Expenses of Management .	
		Commission	
Other Receipts to be specified		Other Payments to be specified	
		Amount of Fire Insurance Fund at the end of the year, as per Fourth Schedule	
£		£	

Note.—When Marine or any other branch of business is carried on, the income and expenditure thereof to be in like manner stated in a separate account.

No. 3.—PROFIT AND LOSS ACCOUNT.

Balance of last year's Account..............		Dividends and Bonuses to Shareholders..............	
Interest and Dividends not carried to other Accounts		Expenses not charged to other Accounts...........	
Profit realised (accounts to be specified)		Loss realised(accounts to be specified)	
Other Receipts...............		Other Payments	
		Balance as per Fourth Schedule	
£		£	

Note.—This account is not required if the items have been incorporated in the other accounts of this Schedule.

FOURTH SCHEDULE.

BALANCE SHEET of the   on the   18

LIABILITIES.	£ s. d.	ASSETS.	£ s. d.
Shareholders' Capital...............		Mortgages on Property within the	
General Reserve Fund (if any)...		United Kingdom..................	
Life Assurance Fund *		Do. out of the United Kingdom...	
Annuity Fund (if any)*...........		Loans on the Company's Policies	
Fire Fund		Investments—	
Marine Fund		In British Government Securities	
Profit and Loss (if any)...........		Indian and Colonial do.	
Other Funds (if any, to be speci-		Foreign do.	
fied)		Railway and other Debentures	
	£ s. d.	and Debenture Stocks	
Claims under Life Poli-		Do. Shares (Preference and	
cies admitted, but not		Ordinary)	
yet paid *...............		House Property.................	
Outstanding Fire Losses		Other Investments (to be	
Do. Marine Losses		specified)	
Other Sums owing by		Loans upon Personal Security ...	
the Company (Ac-		Agents' Balances....................	
counts to be specified)		Outstanding Premiums	
		Do. Interest...........................	
		Cash—On Deposit ....£	
		In hand and on Cur-	
		rent Account......	
		Other Assets (to be specified) ...	
	£		£

* If the Life Assurance Fund is, in accordance with Section 4 of this Act,
a separate trust fund for the sole security of the Life Policy holders, a
separate Balance Sheet for the Life Branch may be given in the form contained in Schedule 2. In other respects the Company is to observe the above
form. See also note to Second Schedule.

FIFTH SCHEDULE.

STATEMENT RESPECTING THE VALUATION OF THE LIABILITIES UNDER LIFE
     POLICIES AND ANNUITIES of the
     to be made by the Actuary.

(The answers should be numbered to accord with the numbers of the corresponding questions.)

1. The date up to which the valuation is made.

2. The principles upon which the valuation and distribution of profits
among the Policy-holders are made, and whether these principles were determined by the instrument constituting the Company, or by its Regulations or
Bye-laws, or otherwise.

3. The Table or Tables of Mortality used in the valuation.

4. The Rate or Rates of Interest assumed in the calculations.

5. The proportion of the Annual Premium Income (if any) reserved as a

provision for future expenses and profits. (If none, state how this provision is made.)

6. The Consolidated Revenue Account since the last valuation, or, in case of a Company which has made no valuation, since the commencement of the business. (This return should be made in the Form annexed.)

7. The liabilities of the Company under Life Policies and Annuities at the date of the valuation, showing the number of Policies, the amount assured, and the amount of Premiums payable annually under each class of Policies, both with and without participation in profits; and also the net liabilities and assets of the Company, with the amount of surplus or deficiency. (These returns should be made in the Form annexed.)

8. The time during which a Policy must be in force in order to entitle it to share in the profits.

9. The results of the valuation, showing—

(1.) The total amount of profit made by the Company.

(2.) The amount of profit divided among the Policy-holders, and the number and amount of the Policies which participated.

(3.) Specimens of Bonuses allotted to Policies for £100 effected at the respective ages of 20, 30, 40, and 50, and having been respectively in force for five years, ten years, and upwards, at intervals of five years respectively, together with the amounts apportioned under the various modes in which the Bonus might be received.

(FORM referred to under heading No. 6, in the Fifth Schedule.)

CONSOLIDATED REVENUE ACCOUNT of the   for   years
                commencing   and ending

	£ s. d.		£ s. d.
Amount of Funds on 18 , the beginning of		Claims under Policies (after deduction of sums Re-assured)...	
Premiums (after deduction of Re-assurance Premiums)		Surrenders	
Consideration for Annuities granted		Annuities	
Interest and Dividends		Commission	
Other Receipts (accounts to be specified)		Expenses of Management	
		Dividends and Bonuses to Share-holders (if any)	
		Other Payments (accounts to be specified)	
		Amount of Funds on 18 , the end of the period, as per First (or Third) Schedule	
£		£	

(FORM referred to under heading No. 7 in Fifth Schedule.)

SUMMARY AND VALUATION OF THE POLICIES of the   as at   18

DESCRIPTION OF TRANSACTIONS.	Number of Policies.	Sums assured and Bonuses.	Office Yearly Premiums.	Net Yearly Premiums, if ascertained.	Sums Assured and Bonuses.	Office Yearly Premiums.	Net Yearly Premiums, if computed.	Net Liability.
		PARTICULARS OF THE POLICIES FOR VALUATION.			VALUATION.			
					Value by the Interest		Table, per Cent.	
ASSURANCES.								
I. *With participation in Profits.*								
For whole term of life								
Other Classes (to be specified)......								
Extra Premiums payable								
Total Assurances with Profits								
II. *Without participation in Profits.*								
For whole term of life								
Other Classes (to be specified)......								
Extra Premiums payable								
Total Assurances without Profits								
Total Assurances								
Deduct Re-assurances								
Net Amount of Assurances ...								
Adjustments (if any)...........								
ANNUITIES.								
Immediate								
Other Classes (to be specified)......								
Total of the Results								

The term " extra Premium " in this Act shall be taken to mean the charge for any risk not provided for in the Minimum Contract Premium. If Policies are issued in or for any country at Rates of Premium deduced from Tables other than the European Mortality Tables adopted by the Company, separate Schedules similar in form to the above must be furnished.

(FORM referred to under heading No. 7 in Fifth Schedule.)

VALUATION BALANCE SHEET of   as at   18 .

Dr.   Cr.

	£			£
To Net Liability under Assurance and Annuity Transactions (as per Summary Statement provided in Schedule 5)............		By Life Assurance and Annuity Funds (as per Balance Sheet under Schedule 2 or 4)		
„ Surplus (if any)		„ Deficiency (if any)		
	£			£

SIXTH SCHEDULE.

STATEMENT OF THE LIFE ASSURANCE AND ANNUITY BUSINESS of the
on the   18

(The answers should be numbered to accord with the numbers of the corresponding questions. Statements of Re-assurances corresponding to the statements in respect of Assurances under headings 2, 3, 4, 5, and 6, are to be given.)

1. The published Table or Tables of Premiums for Assurances for the whole term of life which are in use at the date above mentioned.

2. The total amount Assured on lives for the whole term of life, which are in existence at the date above mentioned, distinguishing the portions Assured with and without Profits, stating separately the total Reversionary Bonuses, and specifying the sums Assured for each year of life from the youngest to the oldest ages.

3. The amount of Premiums receivable annually for each year of life, after deducting the abatements made by the application of Bonuses, in respect of the respective Assurances mentioned under heading No. 2, distinguishing ordinary from extra Premiums.

4. The total amount Assured under classes of Assurance Business other than for the whole term of life, distinguishing the sums Assured under each class, and stating separately the amount Assured with and without Profits, and the total amount of Reversionary Bonuses.

5. The amount of Premiums receivable annually in respect of each such special class of Assurances mentioned under heading No. 4, distinguishing ordinary from extra Premiums.

6. The total amount of Premiums which has been received from the commencement upon all Policies under each special class mentioned under heading No. 4, which are in force at the date above mentioned.

7. The total amount of immediate Annuities on lives, distinguishing the amounts for each year of life.

8. The amount of all Annuities other than those specified under heading No. 7, distinguishing the amount of Annuities payable under each class, the amount of Premiums annually receivable, and the amount of consideration-money received in respect of each such class, and the total amount of Premiums received from the commencement upon all Deferred Annuities.

9. The average rate of Interest at which the Life Assurance Fund of the Company was invested at the close of each year during the period since the last investigation.

10. A Table of Minimum Values, if any, allowed for the surrender of Policies for the whole term of life, and for Endowments and Endowment Assurances, or a statement of the method pursued in calculating such Surrender Values, with instances of its application to Policies of different standing, and taken out at various interval ages from the youngest to the oldest.

Separate statements to be furnished for business at other than European rates, together with a statement of the manner in which Policies on unhealthy lives are dealt with.

FRIENDLY SOCIETIES ACT, 1875.

38 & 39 Vict., c. 60.

ANNUAL RETURN AS PRESCRIBED BY THE CHIEF REGISTRAR.

Forms A and B.

RETURNS REQUIRED FROM A REGISTERED SOCIETY

(Not being a Collecting Society within S. 30 of the Act).

Year ending 31st December, 18 .

[*The Society's Balance Sheet cannot be accepted as a substitute for this Return.*]

This Return is to be sent to the Registrar before the 1st of June, 18 .

A copy of the Auditors' Report (if any) should also be sent.

Name of Society

Register No. . [*Add* Scotland *or* Ireland, *where necessary.*]

Date of commencement of Society 18 .

When first Enrolled, Certified, or Registered

Names of the present Trustees

Name and Address of the Treasurer and of any }
  other Officer in receipt or charge of money }

Amount of Security given by him or them ... ... £_____

Number of Benefit Members at the beginning of the year ...

Number of Benefit Members admitted during the year ...

                                 Together _____

Number of Benefit Members who died during the year ... }
Number of Benefit Members who left from other causes ... }

Total Number of Benefit Members at the end of the year ...

Average amount of Funds per Member [that is, the total
  Funds on the 31st December, 18 , divided by the total
  number of Benefit Members] ... ... £

State what provision (if any) is made for old age

The Audit for the year has been conducted by Mr. , Public
Auditor * [*or* by of
whose calling or profession is , and
of , whose calling or profession is
who were appointed Auditors by under the
authority of Rule No.].

Registered Office of the Society † in the county
of

      Date 18 .

This portion is to be filled up whether Form A or Form B is adopted.

---

  * This term means only a Public Auditor appointed under the Friendly
Societies Act.

  † State full postal address.

FORM A.—FOR SOCIETIES WHOSE MEMBERS PAY ONLY ONE CONTRIBUTION FOR ALL BENEFITS.

BENEFIT FUND.

Receipts.

	£ s. d.
Contributions	
Levies (if any)	
[If for more than one purpose, state on separate lines the amount raised for each.]	
Fines (not appropriated to Management Fund) ...	
Entrance Fees (not appropriated to Management Fund) ...	
Interest on Investments of Benefit Fund...	
Other Receipts (a)	
(a) Specify their nature.	
Total Receipts	
Amount of Benefit Fund at the beginning of the year 18 ...	
Total	£

Expenditure.

Sums at Death.   Sickness Pay.

	£ s. d. £ s. d. £ s. d.
weeks pay to Members on full pay (lasting by Rules weeks) ...	
weeks pay to Members on reduced pay (1st period, lasting weeks) ..	
weeks pay to Members on reduced pay (2nd period, lasting weeks) (e)	
of Members and Children of Members *above 10 years of age* ...	
of [Wives or Husbands] of Members ...	
of Children *under 5 years of age* ...	
of Children *between 5 and 10 years of age* ...	
of age	
(e) If any further reductions they should be stated separately.	
Cost of Medical Aid, if not paid out of Management Fund	
Payments for other Benefits (if any) (f)...	
Other Payments (if any) (g) ...	
(f) State separately the expenditure for each.	
(g) Specify their nature.	
Total Expenditure ...	
Amount of Benefit Fund at the end of the year 18 , as per Balance Sheet (below) ...	
Total	£

MANAGEMENT FUND.*

* If the Society was registered before 23rd July, 1855, and has no separate Management Fund provided for in its Rules, state the fact.

Receipts.

	£ s. d.
Donations of Honorary Members to this Fund ...	
Contributions of Members for Management ...	
Levies upon Members for Management ...	
Fines appropriated to this Fund by the Society's Rules	
Entrance Fees do. do. ...	
Interest on Investments of Management Fund ...	
Other Receipts (if any) (b)...	
(b) Specify their nature	
Total Receipts	
Amount of Management Fund at the beginning of the year 18	
Total	£

Expenditure.

	£ s. d. £ s. d.
Salaries	
Rent	
Printing, Stationery, and Postage ...	
Other Payments (if any) (h) ...	
(h) Specify their nature.	
Total Expenses of Management	
Bad Debts and Losses ...	
Cost of Medical Aid, if paid out of this Fund	
Total Expenditure	
Amount of Management Fund at the end of the year 18 , as per Balance Sheet (below) ...	
Total	£

	£	s.	d.			£	s.	d.	
Amount of Benefit Fund (as above)		...		Investments—					
Amount of Management Fund (as above)		...		1. In the Saving's Bank, yielding interest at per cent.					(i) State amount and description of stock.
Debts (if any) legally incurred by Trustees on behalf of the Society (c)		...		2. In the Public Funds (i)					
Cash due to Treasurer (if any)		...		3. With the Commissioners for the Reduction of the National Debt, yielding interest at per cent.					
Other Liabilities (d)		...		4. Upon Government Securities in Great Britain or Ireland, yielding interest at per cent. ...					
				5. Upon Real Securities in Great Britain or Ireland, yielding interest at an average of per cent...					
(c) Specify their nature.				6. In the Purchase of Land					(k) If on the securities state them separately.
(d) Specify them.				7. In the Erection of Offices and Buildings					(l) State in whose hands.
				8. In (k)					(m) Specify them.
				Cash in the Post Office Saving's Bank ...					
				Cash in hand (l)					
				Other Assets (if any) (m)					
Total ...	£			Total ...	£				

Signature of Treasurer or one of the Trustees

Signature of Secretary   Residing at *

         * Give Postal Address.

The undersigned, having had access to all the Books and Accounts of the Society, and having examined the foregoing General Statement, and verified the same with the Accounts and Vouchers relating thereto, now sign the same as found to be correct, duly vouched, and in accordance with law.

     * Public Auditor: or   and   Auditors.

* This term means only a Public Auditor appointed under the Friendly Societies Act.

Date   18 .

If in any respect these Accounts are incorrect, unvouched, or not in accordance with law, the *Auditors are not to sign as above*, but are to make a Special Report to the Society, of which a copy is to be sent to the Registrar with this Statement.

N.B.—Societies to which this Form applies need not fill up Form A.

FORM B.—FOR SOCIETIES WHOSE MEMBERS PAY MORE THAN ONE CONTRIBUTION FOR BENEFITS.

BENEFIT FUNDS.

Receipts.

	£	s.	d.
Entrance Fees (not appropriated to Management Fund) ...			
Contributions (a) for Sickness (b) ...			
Contributions for Sums at Death (b) ...			
Contributions for Annuities ...			
Contributions for Endowments ...			
Contributions for Old Age Pay [where separate] ...			
Contributions for Widows and Orphans' Allowances [where separate] ...			
Contributions for Lying-in [where separate]...			
Contributions for Accidents [where separate] ...			
Contributions for Travelling Benefit [where separate] ...			
Contributions for Distress Relief [where separate] ...			
Contributions for Medical Aid [where separate] ...			
Contributions to Separate Loan Fund [under s. 18 (2) of Act] ...			
Contributions for (e) ...			
Contributions for ...			
Contributions for ...			
Fines not appropriated to Management Fund .			
Interest on Investments of Benefit Funds ...			
Other Receipts (if any) (d) ...			
Total Receipts ...			
Amount of Benefit Funds at the beginning of the year ...			
Total £			

(a) Where levies are made for benefits, in addition to the contributions, the contributions and levies for each benefit should be separately stated. Where a single contribution provides for more than one benefit the lines may be bracketed together.

(b) If under more than one Table, the amount under each Table should be separately stated.

(c) Other benefits (if any) for which separate contributions are paid, should be stated separately.

(d) Specify their nature.

Expenditure.

Sums at Death. / Sickness Pay.

	£	s.	d.	£	s.	d.
weeks pay to Members on full pay (lasting by Rules weeks)						
weeks pay to Members on reduced pay (1st period lasting weeks)						
weeks pay to Members on reduced pay (2nd period lasting weeks (h)) .						
of Members and Children of Members above 10 years of age ...						
of Wives [or Husbands] of Members						
of Children under 5 years of age ...						
of Children between 5 and 10 years of age ...						
Annuities...						
Endowments ...						
Old Age Pay ...						
Widows and Orphans' Allowances ...						
Lying-in Pay ...						
Accident Allowances ...						
Travelling Benefit ...						
Distress Relief ...						
Cost of Medical Aid (if paid out of a separate fund) ...						
Loans out of Separate Loan Fund [under s.18(2) of Act] *This amount must not be included in total expenditure.*						
Payments for other Benefits (if any) (i) ...						
Other Payments (if any) (k) ...						
Total Expenditure ...						
Amount of Benefit Funds at the end of the year, as per Balance Sheet (below) ...						
Total £						

(h) If any further deductions they should be stated separately.

(i) State separately the expenditure for each.

(k) Specify their nature.

MANAGEMENT FUND.*

Receipts.

	£	s.	d.
Donations of Honorary Members appropriated to this Fund ...			
Contributions of Members for Management ...			
Levies upon Members for Management			

Expenditure.

	£	s.	d.
Salaries ...			
Rent ...			
Printing, Stationery, and Postages ...			
Other Payments (if any) (l) ...			

(l) Specify...

* If the Society was registered before 23rd July, 1855, and has no separate Management Fund provided for in its Rules, state the fact.

Interest on Investments (if any)
(d) Specify their Other Receipts (if any) (d) ... ...
nature.   Total Receipts   ... ...
Amount of Management Fund at the begin-
ning of the year   ...   ...   Total £

Total Expenditure   ...   ...
Amount of Management Fund at the end of the
year, as per Balance Sheet (below)   ...
Total £

Dr.		£ s. d.		Cr.		£ s. d.

BALANCE SHEET OF FUNDS AND EFFECTS.

(e) Where a single contribution provides more than one benefit, the lines may be bracketed together.

Amount of Sickness Fund (e) ... ...
Amount of Death Fund... ... ...
Amount of Annuity Fund   ... ...
Amount of Endowment Fund ... ...
Amount of Old Age Fund [where separate] ...
Amount of Widows and Orphans' Fund [where separate] ... ...
Amount of Lying-in Fund [where separate] ...
Amount of Accident Fund [where separate] ...
Amount of Travelling Benefit Fund [where separate] ... ...
Amount of District Relief Fund [where separate]
Amount of Medical Aid Fund [where separate]
Amount of Surplus Fund accumulated for Members' use, under s. 19 of Act. ...
Amount of Separate Loan Fund, under s. 18 (2) of Act ... ...

[If there are other benefit funds, state each separately.]

Amount of   ...   .
Amount of   ...   .
             Total Benefit Funds (as above) ...
Amount of Management Fund (as above) ...

(f) Specify their nature.

Debts (if any) (f) legally incurred by Trustees on behalf of the Society   ...
Cash due to Treasurer (if any)   ...

(g) Specify them.

Other liabilities (if any) (g) ...   ...
             Total £

Investments:
1. In the   Saving's Bank, interest at
   per cent.   ...   .
2. In the Public Funds (m)   ...   .
3. With the Commissioners for the Reduction of the National Debt, interest at per cent.
4. Upon Government Securities in Great Britain or Ireland, interest at per cent. ...
5. Upon Real Securities in Great Britain or Ireland, interest at an average of per cent.
6. In the Purchase of Land   ...   .
7. In the Erection of Offices and Buildings ...
8. In Loans on Members' Assurances, under s. 18 (1) of Act, interest at per cent. ...
9. In Loans out of Separate Loan Fund, under s. 18 (2) of Act, interest at per cent. ...
10. In other Securities (n)   ...   .

Cash in the Post Office Saving's Bank ...
Cash in hand (o) ...   .
Other Assets (if any) (p)   ...   .
             Total £

(m) State amount and description of stock.

(n) State them separately.

(o) State in whose hands.
(p) Specify them.

Signature of Treasurer or one of the Trustees   Signature of Secretary   Residing at*   *State Postal Address.

The undersigned, having had access to all the Books and Accounts of the Society, and having examined the foregoing General Statement, and verified the same with the Accounts and Vouchers relating thereto, now sign the same as found to be correct, duly vouched, and in accordance with law.

and

*Public Auditor; or   Auditors.   Date   188

* This term means only a Public Auditor appointed under the Friendly Societies Act.

If in any respect these Accounts are incorrect, unvouched, or not in accordance with law, the *Auditors are not to sign as above*, but are to make a Special Report to the Society, of which a copy is to be sent to the Registrar with this Statement.

RECEIPTS AND EXPENDITURE ACCOUNT (PRO FORMÂ) OF A MINING COMPANY.

Particulars of Receipts.	Receipts previous to period under Audit. £ s. d.	Receipts for period under Audit. £ s. d.	Total Receipts to date. £ s. d.	Particulars of Expenditure.	Expenditure previous to period under Audit. £ s. d.	Expenditure for period under Audit. £ s. d.	Total Expenditure to date. £ s. d.
Shareholders' Capital				Purchase of Mine, Buildings, Plant, &c.			
Mortgagees				Plant and Machinery			
Debentures				Wages			
Sales				Royalties			
Freight and Wagons				Stores			
Transfer Fees				Directors' Fees, Salaries, and Office Expenses			
				Furniture, Fittings, Fixtures, &c.			
				Freight, Carriage, &c.			
				Wagon Hire and Instalments on Wagons on Purchase Lease			
				Interest on Mortgages and Debentures			
				Dividends to Shareholders			
				Preliminary Expenses			
				Balance at Bankers and in hand			

Revenue Account (Pro Forma) of a Mining Company.

Divided into three Sections, as recommended on page 108.

	£	s.	d.		£	s.	d.
To Stock on hand (at commencement of period)...				By Sales			
„ Stores on hand (at commencement of period)...				„ Stock of Coal on hand (at end of period)			
„ Wages........................				„ Stores on hand (at end of period).....................			
„ Royalties.....................							
„ Stores purchased							
„ Balance carried down, being the gross Profit .							
„ Directors' Fees				„ Balance brought down ...			
„ Salaries				„ Transfer Fees...............			
„ Rent, Rates, &c.				„ Extra Earnings of Wagons (including proportion of instalments paid on Wagons on Purchase Lease charged against Revenue).................			
„ Office Expenses							
„ Interest on Mortgages ...							
„ Interest on Debentures...							
„ Amount written off for Depreciation on Buildings, Plant, &c.							
„ Bad Debts							
„ Amount written off Preliminary Expenses Account							
„ Balance carried down, being the net Profit for the period				„ Balance carried down, being the net Loss for the period			
„ Balance brought down, being the net Loss for the period				„ Balance brought down, being the net Profit for the period			
„ Balance brought from previous Revenue Account (deficiency at that date)				„ Balance brought from previous Revenue Account (surplus at that date)			
„ Interim Dividend							
„ Proposed Dividend at per cent. per annum ...							
To Balance carried to Balance Sheet, being amount of Undivided Profit at end of the period				„ Balance carried to Balance Sheet, being deficiency at this date ...			

Balance Sheet (Pro Formâ) of a Mining Company.

	£ s. d.	£ s. d.		£ s. d.	£ s. d.	£ s. d.
To Capital—			By Debtors ...			
Authorised issue—			,, Bills receivable on hand ...			
...... Shares of £... each : £......			,, Cash at Bankers ...			
Subscribed—			,, Cash in hand ...			
...... Shares ...			,, Stock of Coal, at cost price ...			
Less Amount uncalled ...			,, Colliery Stores do. ...			
,, Calls in arrear ...			,, Office Furniture ...			
,, Mortgagees...			,, Purchase of Colliery, Buildings, Plant, &c.—			
,, Debenture Holders...			Balance of this Account ...			
,, Creditors—			Additions to do. ...			
On Open Accounts ...			Less per cent. written off for depreciation			
,, Bills Payable ...						
,, Shareholders' Interest—			,, Instalments on Wagons, on Purchase Lease, after deducting amount charged against Revenue Account			
Outstanding ...			,, Preliminary Expenses—			
,, Balance brought from Revenue Account, being the surplus or amount of Un-divided Profit at this date			Balance of this Account			
			Less th of original Amount			
			,, Balance brought from Revenue Account, being the deficiency at this date ...			

APPENDIX B.

FORM REQUIRED TO BE MADE ANNUALLY BY EVERY COM-
PANY REGISTERED UNDER THE COMPANIES ACT,
1862, HAVING A CAPITAL DIVIDED INTO SHARES.

FORM OF STATEMENT REQUIRED TO BE MADE TWICE
A YEAR BY EVERY LIMITED BANKING OR INSURANCE
COMPANY, AND EVERY DEPOSIT, PROVIDENT, OR
BENEFIT SOCIETY, REGISTERED UNDER THE COM-
PANIES ACT, 1862.

FORM OF STATEMENT PRESCRIBED BY THE INDUSTRIAL
AND PROVIDENT SOCIETIES ACT, 1876, FOR EVERY
SOCIETY CARRYING ON THE BUSINESS OF BANKING.

EXTRACTS FROM THE CONDITIONS UNDER WHICH PUBLIC
AUDITORS HOLD THEIR APPOINTMENTS UNDER THE
FRIENDLY SOCIETIES ACTS, AND THE INDUSTRIAL
AND PROVIDENT SOCIETIES ACT, 1876.

TABLE FOR ASCERTAINING THE AMOUNT TO BE WRITTEN
OFF A LEASE ACCOUNT ANNUALLY, IN ORDER TO
EXHAUST THE SAME AT THE EXPIRATION OF THE
LEASE, ALSO FOR ASCERTAINING THE PRESENT VALUE
OF A LEASE.

LEDGER ACCOUNT (PRO FORMÂ) OF A LEASE FROM DATE
OF PURCHASE UNTIL ITS EXPIRATION.

THE COMPANIES ACT, 1862.

FORM E, AS REQUIRED BY THE SECOND PART OF THE ACT.

(Section 26, Page 18.)

SUMMARY OF CAPITAL AND SHARES of the   COMPANY, made up to the   day of

     Nominal Capital £   divided into   Shares of £   each.

     Number of Shares taken up to the   day of

     There has been called up on each Share £

     Total Amount of Calls received £

     Total Amount of Calls unpaid £

List of Persons holding Shares in the   Company on the   day of

Shares thereon at any Time during the Year immediately preceding the said   day of   , and of Persons who have held

Addresses, and an Account of the Shares so held.   , showing their Names and

Folio in Register Ledger containing Particulars.	NAMES, ADDRESSES, AND OCCUPATIONS.			Shares held by existing Members on the day of	ACCOUNT OF SHARES.				Remarks.
	Surname.	Christian Name.	Address.	Occupation.		Additional Shares held by existing Members during preceding Year.		Shares held by Persons no longer Members.	
						Number.	Date of Transfer.	Number.	Date of Transfer.

THE COMPANIES ACT, 1862.

FORM OF STATEMENT (or as near thereto as circumstances will admit) to be made by every Limited Banking Company, Insurance Company, and Deposit, Provident, or Benefit Society, under this Act, before they commence business, and the first Monday in February and August, and a copy of which has to be put up in a conspicuous place in the registered office and in every branch office or place of business.

* The Capital of the Company is　　　　　　　　divided into Shares of　　　　　　each.

The number of Shares issued is

Calls to the amount of　　　　　　pounds per Share have been made, under which the sum of　　　　　　pounds has been received.

The liabilities of the Company on the first day of January (or July) were—

Debts owing to Sundry persons by the Company
　　　On judgment £
　　　On specialty £
　　　On notes or bills £
　　　On simple contracts £
　　　On estimated liabilities £

The Assets of the Company on that day were—
　　　Government Securities [stating them], £
　　　Bills of Exchange and Promissory Notes, £
　　　Cash at the Bankers, £
　　　Other Securities, £

---

* If the Company has no Capital divided into Shares, the portion of the Statement relating to Capital and Shares must be omitted.

THE INDUSTRIAL AND PROVIDENT SOCIETIES ACT, 1876.

FORM OF STATEMENT TO BE MADE OUT BY A SOCIETY CARRYING ON THE BUSINESS OF BANKING.

(See Section 10, Page 74.)

1. Capital of the Society :—
　(a.) Amount of each Share.
　(b.) Number of Shares issued.
　(c.) Amount paid up on Shares.

2. Liabilities of the Society on the first day of January (or July) last previous :—
　(a.) On judgments.
　(b.) On specialty.
　(c.) On notes or bills.
　(d.) On simple contract.
　(e.) On estimated liabilities.

3. Assets of the Society on the same date :—
　(a.) Government Securities (stating them).
　(b.) Bills of Exchange and Promissory Notes.
　(c.) Cash at the bankers.
　(d.) Other securities.

EXTRACTS from the Conditions under which Public Auditors will hold their appointment under the Friendly Societies Acts, and the Industrial and Provident Societies Act, 1876.

(Prescribed by Her Majesty's Treasury.)

1. The country will be divided into districts, and Public Auditors for each district appointed. They will not, however, be ranked as public servants, and will have no salaries, nor any claim to pension or gratuity. Public Auditors are not permitted to make use of the Royal Arms.

2. The Public Auditor is bound to accept for audit (except as hereinafter mentioned) the accounts of any society within his district which applies to him (the term " Society " to include a branch of a society), at the scale of fees hereafter mentioned, the society complying with the terms of these instructions. But no Public Auditor can audit the accounts, balance-sheet, or annual return of any society of which he is accountant, or any account, balance-sheet, or annual return which he has himself prepared.

3. A society desirous of submitting its accounts to a Public Auditor must forward all the necessary materials to his office or place of residence, in order to save travelling expenses and loss of time. It will be the duty of the Auditor, when applied to, to impress this upon the society. He is not bound to leave his office for the purpose of the audit.

4. The society must, at the same time, forward to the Auditor the annual return or general statement of the receipts and expenditure funds and effects of the society, made up in the form for the time being required under the Friendly Societies Act, 1875 [or the Industrial and Provident Societies Act, 1876], as the case may be.

5. The Auditor is to verify the annual return with the accounts and vouchers relating thereto, and either to sign the same as found by him to be correct, duly vouched, and in accordance with law, or specially to report to the society in what respects he finds it incorrect, unvouched, or not in accordance with law.

6. The work of the Auditor will be strictly confined to auditing, but he has under the Acts a right of access to all the books and accounts of the society. In the event of his discovering errors in the annual return, or the books, accounts, or vouchers submitted to him, they are to be returned (at the cost of the society) for correction, unless the Auditor be requested by the society to correct the inaccuracies, in which case he is entitled to claim an additional fee, to be arranged between him and the society.

7. The Auditor shall, in all cases, make a report to the society upon the accounts and other documents submitted to him, and, in case he has called for explanations or information from the Directors or Committee of Management, he shall state whether such explanations or information have been given, and whether they have been satisfactory.

8. Rates of payment :—

(1.) For auditing the accounts of Friendly Societies the scale of payment shall be—

	£	s.	d.
For societies consisting of not more than 100 members	1	1	0
For societies with over 100 members, but not exceeding 500 members, in respect of each 100 members or part thereof	1	1	0
For societies consisting of over 500 members in respect of the first 500 members	5	5	0

With an additional 10*s.* 6*d.* in respect of each additional 100 members or part thereof. No fee, however, to exceed £52 10*s.* unless by special arrangement.

*   *   *   *

9. The scales of fees apply only in cases where the Society is located within the district assigned to the Auditor employed. If a society employs an Auditor appointed for any other district, special terms may be arranged.

The Auditor may accept audits on terms lower than those of the above scale.

10. Auditors shall hold their appointments from year to year, beginning on the first day of January in each year. The Treasury reserves to itself entire discretion as to reappointing them.

11. They shall send in half yearly to the Treasury a list containing the names of the societies audited by them during the previous half year, and the fees received from each society, distinguishing societies under the Friendly Societies Acts from societies under the Industrial and Provident Societies Acts.

12. The scales of fees above laid down will only remain in force from year to year. At the end of any year they may be confirmed or altered in such manner as the Treasury may direct.

13. Auditors are requested to make themselves acquainted with the provisions of the Friendly Societies Acts, and of the Industrial and Provident Societies Act, 1876, which affect the exercise of their functions. Their attention is particularly directed to Sections 14 and 32 of the Friendly Societies Act, 1875, and to Sections 10 and 18 of the Industrial and Provident Societies Act, 1876.

———

The principal points to be attended to in filling up the return are—

1. That in each account the amount of the fund at the beginning of the year must be the same as that at the end of the year in the previous year's return.

2. That each account be correctly added up.

3. The totals at the bottom on the opposite sides of each account to be the same.

4. That the return be signed by all the officers required, including the Auditors, if they find the accounts correct.

5. That the funds of the Society are invested in strict accordance with the Registered Rules of the Society. The investment of monies on notes of hand and other personal securities, is not legal.

6. Investments made should not be put down as *expenditure,* nor investments sold or repaid put down as *receipts.*

That all receipts and expenditure outside the objects of the Society, such as for banners, fêtes, anniversaries, &c., be *not* included in the Return.

TABLE.

For ascertaining the amount to be charged annually against the Revenue Account and written off a Lease Account in order to exhaust the same at the expiration of such Lease, with interest at 3, 4, 5, 6, 7, 8, 9, or 10 per cent. per annum.

Also for ascertaining the value of a Lease at the above several rates of interest.

The rate per cent. is of course contingent upon many circumstances, but it may be a guide to state that in cases of compensation the Metropolitan Board of Works allow interest to be calculated at the rate of 6 per cent. per annum.

EXAMPLES.

1. A Company purchases the seven years Lease of its business premises for £3476 10s.

Required the sum which should be charged annually against the Revenue Account until the expiration of the Lease.

Interest at 6 per cent. per annum.

£3476 10s. = £3476·5.

Divide 3476·5 by 5·582, the number in the 6 per cent. column on the same line with 7 in the years' column in the table. This gives 622·805, or £622 16s. 1d., the sum required.

The Lease Account as it should appear in the Ledger is given on p. 198.

2. A Lease for fourteen years to make 7 per cent. and to get back the Principal is worth 8·745 or 8¾ years' purchase of the Clear Annual Rent.

The Clear Annual Rent is ascertained by deducting from the estimated or improved Rent the reserved Rent, if any, and all Taxes and other annual charges.

TABLE.

Years.	Years Purchase.								Years.
	3 per cent.	4 per cent.	5 per cent.	6 per cent.	7 per cent.	8 per cent.	9 per cent.	10 per cent.	
½	·489	·485	·482	·479	·475	·472	·469	·465	½
1	·971	·962	·952	·943	·935	·926	·917	·909	1
1½	1·446	1·428	1·411	1·395	1·379	1·363	1·347	1·332	1½
2	1·913	1·886	1·859	1·833	1·808	1·783	1·759	1·736	2
2½	2·374	2·335	2·297	2·259	2·223	2·188	2·154	2·120	2½
3	2·829	2·775	2·723	2·673	2·624	2·577	2·531	2·487	3
3½	3·276	3·207	3·140	3·075	3·012	2·952	2·893	2·836	3½
4	3·717	3·630	3·546	3·465	3·387	3·312	3·240	3·170	4
4½	4·152	4·045	3·942	3·844	3·750	3·659	3·572	3·488	4½
5	4·580	4·452	4·329	4·212	4·100	3·993	3·890	3·791	5
5½	5·002	4·851	4·707	4·570	4·439	4·314	4·194	4·080	5½
6	5·417	5·242	5·076	4·917	4·767	4·623	4·486	4·355	6
6½	5·827	5·626	5·435	5·255	5·083	4·920	4·765	4·618	6½
7	6·230	6·002	5·786	5·582	5·389	5·206	5·033	4·868	7
7½	6·628	6·371	6·129	5·901	5·685	5·482	5·289	5·107	7½
8	7·020	6·733	6·463	6·210	5·971	5·747	5·535	5·335	8
8½	7·406	7·087	6·789	6·510	6·248	6·002	5·770	5·552	8½
9	7·776	7·435	7·108	6·802	6·515	6·247	5·995	5·759	9
9½	8·161	7·776	7·419	7·085	6·774	6·483	6·211	5·956	9½
10	8·530	8·111	7·722	7·360	7·024	6·710	6·418	6·145	10
10½	8·894	8·439	8·018	7·627	7·265	6·929	6·616	6·324	10½
11	9·253	8·760	8·306	7·887	7·499	7·139	6·805	6·495	11
11½	9·606	9·076	8·588	8·139	7·724	7·341	6·987	6·658	11½
12	9·954	9·385	8·863	8·384	7·943	7·536	7·161	6·814	12
12½	10·297	9·688	9·132	8·622	8·154	7·723	7·327	6·962	12½
13	10·635	9·986	9·394	8·853	8·358	7·904	7·487	7·103	13
13½	10·968	10·277	9·649	9·077	8·555	8·077	7·640	7·238	13½
14	11·296	10·563	9·899	9·295	8·745	8·244	7·786	7·367	14
14½	11·619	10·843	10·142	9·507	8·930	8·405	7·926	7·489	14½
15	11·938	11·118	10·380	9·712	9·108	8·559	8·061	7·606	15
15½	12·252	11·388	10·612	9·912	9·280	8·708	8·189	7·717	15½
16	12·561	11·652	10·838	10·106	9·447	8·851	8·313	7·824	16
16½	12·866	11·911	11·059	10·294	9·608	8·989	8·431	7·925	16½
17	13·166	12·166	11·274	10·477	9·763	9·122	8·544	8·022	17
17½	13·462	12·415	11·484	10·655	9·914	9·249	8·652	8·114	17½
18	13·754	12·659	11·690	10·828	10·059	9·372	8·756	8·201	18
18½	14·041	12·899	11·890	10·995	10·200	9·490	8·855	8·285	18½
19	14·324	13·134	12·085	11·158	10·336	9·604	8·950	8·365	19
19½	14·603	13·364	12·276	11·316	10·467	9·713	9·041	8·441	19½
20	14·877	13·590	12·462	11·470	10·594	9·818	9·129	8·514	20
20½	15·148	13·812	12·644	11·619	10·717	9·919	9·212	8·583	20½
21	15·415	14·029	12·821	11·764	10·836	10·017	9·292	8·649	21
21½	15·678	14·242	12·994	11·905	10·950	10·111	9·369	8·712	21½
22	15·937	14·451	13·163	12·042	11·061	10·201	9·442	8·772	22
22½	16·192	14·656	13·328	12·174	11·168	10·288	9·513	8·829	22½
23	16·444	14·857	13·489	12·303	11·272	10·371	9·580	8·883	23
23½	16·691	15·054	13·645	12·429	11·372	10·451	9·645	8·935	23½
24	16·936	15·247	13·799	12·550	11·469	10·529	9·707	8·985	24
24½	17·176	15·436	13·948	12·669	11·563	10·603	9·766	9·032	24½

TABLE—*continued.*

Years.	YEARS PURCHASE.								Years.
	3 per cent.	4 per cent.	5 per cent.	6 per cent.	7 per cent.	8 per cent.	9 per cent.	10 per cent.	
25	17·413	15·622	14·094	12·783	11·654	10·675	9·823	9·077	25
25½	17·647	15·804	14·236	12·895	11·741	10·744	9·877	9·120	25½
26	17·877	15·983	14·375	13·003	11·826	10·810	9·929	9·161	26
26½	18·104	16·158	14·511	13·108	11·908	10·874	9·979	9·200	26½
27	18·327	16·330	14·643	13·211	11·987	10·935	10·027	9·237	27
27½	18·547	16·498	14·772	13·310	12·063	10·994	10 072	9·273	27½
28	18·764	16·663	14·898	13·406	12·137	11·051	10·116	9·307	28
28½	18·978	16·825	15·021	13·500	12·209	11·106	10·158	9·339	28½
29	19·188	16·984	15·141	13·591	12·278	11·158	10·198	9 370	29
29½	19·396	17·139	15·258	13·679	12·344	11·209	10·237	9·399	29½
30	19·600	17·292	15·372	13·765	12·409	11·258	10·274	9·427	30
30½	19·802	17·442	15·484	13·848	12·471	11·305	10·309	9·454	30½
31	20·300	17·588	15·593	13·929	12·532	11·350	10·343	9 479	31
31½	20·196	17·732	15·699	14·008	12·590	11·393	10·375	9·503	31½
32	20·389	17·874	15·803	14·084	12·647	11·435	10·406	9 526	32
32½	20·579	18·012	15·904	14·158	12·701	11·475	10·436	9·548	32½
33	20 766	18·148	16·003	14·230	12·754	11·514	10·464	9·569	33
33½	20·950	18·281	16·099	14·300	12·805	11·551	10·492	9·589	33½
34	21·132	18·411	16·193	14·368	12·854	11·587	10·518	9·609	34
34½	21·311	18·539	16·285	14·434	12·902	11·621	10·543	9·627	34½
35	21·487	18·665	16·374	14·498	12·948	11·655	10·567	9·644	35
35½	21·661	18·788	16·462	14·561	12·992	11·686	10·590	9·661	35½
36	21·832	18·908	16·547	14·621	13·035	11·717	10·612	9·677	36
36½	22·001	19·027	16·630	14·680	13·077	11·747	10·633	9·692	36½
37	22·167	19·143	16·711	14·737	13·117	11·775	10·653	9·706	37
37½	22·331	19·256	16·791	14·792	13·156	11·803	10·672	9·720	37½
38	22·492	19·368	16·868	14·846	13·193	11·829	10·691	9·733	38
38½	22·652	19·477	16·943	14·898	13·230	11·854	10·709	9·745	38½
39	22·808	19·584	17·017	14·949	13·265	11·879	10·726	9·757	39
39½	22·963	19·690	17·089	14·998	13·299	11·902	10·742	9·768	39½
40	23·115	19·793	17·159	15·046	13·332	11·925	10·757	9·779	40
40½	23·265	19·894	17·228	15·093	13·363	11·946	10·772	9·789	40½
41	23·412	19·993	17·294	15·138	13·394	11·967	10·787	9·799	41
41½	23·558	20·090	17·360	15·182	13·424	11·987	10·800	9·808	41½
42	23·701	20·186	17·423	15·225	13·452	12·007	10·813	9·817	42
42½	23·843	20·279	17·485	15·266	13·480	12·025	10·826	9·826	42½
43	23·982	20·371	17·546	15·306	13·507	12·043	10·838	9·834	43
43½	24·119	20·461	17·605	15·345	13·533	12 060	10·849	9·842	43½
44	24·254	20·549	17·663	15·383	13·558	12·077	10·861	9·849	44
44½	24·387	20·635	17·719	15·420	13·582	12·093	10·871	9·856	44½
45	24·519	20·720	17·774	15·456	13·606	12·108	10·881	9·863	45
45½	24·648	20·803	17·828	15·491	13·628	12·123	10·891	9·869	45½
46	24·775	20·885	17·880	15·524	13·650	12·137	10·900	9·875	46
46½	24·901	20·965	17·931	15·557	13·671	12·151	10·909	9·881	46½
47	25·025	21·043	17·981	15·589	13·692	12·164	10·918	9·887	47
47½	25·147	21·120	18·030	15·620	13·711	12·177	10·926	9·892	47½
48	25·267	21·195	18·077	15·650	13·730	12·189	10·934	9·897	48
48½	25·385	21·269	18·123	15·679	13·749	12·201	10·941	9·902	48½
49	25·502	21·341	18·169	15·708	13·767	12·212	10·948	9·906	49

TABLE—*continued.*

Years.	3 per cent.	4 per cent.	5 per cent.	6 per cent.	7 per cent.	8 per cent.	9 per cent.	10 per cent.	Years.
				Years Purchase.					
49½	25·617	21·413	18·213	15·735	13·784	12·223	10·955	9·911	49½
50	25·730	21·482	18·256	15·762	13·801	12·233	10·962	9·915	50
51	25·951	21·617	18·339	15·813	13·832	12·253	10·974	9·921	51
52	26·166	21·748	18·418	15·861	13·862	12·272	10·985	9·930	52
53	26·375	21·873	18·493	15·907	13·890	12·288	10·996	9·936	53
54	26·578	21·993	18·565	15·950	13·916	12·304	11·005	9·942	54
55	26·774	22·109	18·633	15·991	13·940	12·319	11·014	9·947	55
56	26·965	22·220	18·699	16·029	13·963	12·332	11·022	9·952	56
57	27·151	22·327	18·761	16·065	13·984	12·344	11·029	9·956	57
58	27·331	22·430	18·820	16·099	14·003	12·356	11·036	9·960	58
59	27·506	22·528	18·876	16.131	14·022	12·367	11·042	9·964	59
60	27·676	22·623	18·929	16·161	14·039	12·377	11·048	9·967	60
65	28·453	23·047	19·161	16·289	14·110	12·416	11·070	9·980	65
70	29·123	23·395	19·343	16·385	14·160	12·443	11·084	9·987	70
75	29·702	23·680	19·485	16·456	14·196	12·461	11·094	9·992	75
80	30·201	23·915	19·596	16·509	14·222	12·474	11·100	9·995	80
85	30·631	24·109	19·684	16·549	14·240	12·482	11·104	9·997	85
90	31·002	24·267	19·752	16·579	14·253	12·488	11·106	9·998	90
95	31·323	24·398	19·806	16·601	14·263	12·492	11·108	9·999	95
100	31·599	24·505	19·848	16·618	14·269	12·494	11·109	9·999	100
Perp.	33·333	25·000	20·000	16·667	14·286	12·500	11·111	10·000	Perp.

The Table is taken from the twenty-first edition of " Inwood's Tables," and is printed here with the kind permission of the Publishers, Messrs. Crosby, Lockwood, and Co., 7, Stationers' Hall Court, London, E.C.

LEDGER ACCOUNT of a Seven Years' Lease purchased for £3476 10s. From Date of Purchase to Expiration of the Lease.

(See Explanation of Table, Example 1, page 194.)

Date.		£	s.	d.		£	s.	d.	Date.
Of Purchase. End of 1st year.	To Cash..........	3476	10	0	By Revenue Account	622	16	1	End of 1st year.
	,, Interest at 6 per cent. ...	208	11	9	,, Balance	3062	5	8	
		3685	1	9		3685	1	9	
End of 2nd year.	To Balance	3062	5	8	By Revenue Account	622	16	1	End of 2nd year.
	,, Interest	183	14	8	,, Balance	2623	4	3	
		3246	0	4		3246	0	4	
End of 3rd year.	To Balance	2623	4	3	By Revenue Account	622	16	1	End of 3rd year.
	,, Interest	157	7	10	,, Balance	2157	16	0	
		2780	12	1		2780	12	1	
End of 4th year.	To Balance	2157	16	0	By Revenue Account	622	16	1	End of 4th year.
	,, Interest	129	9	4	,, Balance	1664	9	3	
		2287	5	4		2287	5	4	
End of 5th year.	To Balance	1664	9	3	By Revenue Account	622	16	1	End of 5th year.
	,, Interest	99	17	4	,, Balance	1141	10	6	
		1764	6	7		1764	6	7	
End of 6th year.	To Balance	1141	10	6	By Revenue Account	622	16	1	End of 6th year.
	,, Interest	68	9	9	,, Balance	587	4	2	
		1210	0	3		1210	0	3	
End of 7th year.	To Balance	587	4	2	By Revenue Account	622	8	10	End of 7th year.
	,, Interest	35	4	8					
		622	8	10					

INDEX.

PRINTED BY EFFINGHAM WILSON, ROYAL EXCHANGE.

The History of Accounting

An Arno Press Collection

Bennet[t], James [Arlington]. **The American System of Practical Book-Keeping** and Foster, B[enjamin] F[ranklin], **The Origin and Progress of Book-Keeping.** 1842/1852. Two vols. in one

Brief, Richard P., editor. **The Late Nineteenth Century Debate Over Depreciation, Capital and Income.** 1976

Brief, Richard P. **Nineteenth Century Capital Accounting and Business Investment.** 1976

Bruchey, Stuart W[eems]. **Robert Oliver and Mercantile Bookkeeping in the Early Nineteenth Century.** 1976

Church, A[lexander] Hamilton. **Production Factors in Cost Accounting and Works Management.** 1910

Cole, William Morse. **Accounts:** Their Construction and Interpretation for Business Men and Students of Affairs. 1908

Dicksee, Lawrence R[obert]. **Advanced Accounting.** 1903

Dicksee, Lawrence R[obert]. **Auditing:** A Practical Manual for Auditors. 1892

Dicksee, Lawrence R[obert]. **Auditing:** A Practical Manual for Auditors. Authorized American Edition, Edited by Robert H. Montgomery. 1905

Dicksee, Lawrence R[obert]. **Depreciation, Reserves, and Reserve Funds.** 1903

Dicksee, Lawrence R[obert] and Frank Tillyard. **Goodwill and Its Treatment in Accounts.** 1906

Folsom, E[zekiel] G[ilman]. **Folsom's Logical Bookkeeping:** The Logic of Accounts. 1873

Garcke, Emile and J[ohn] M[anger] Fells. **Factory Accounts, Their Principles and Practice.** 1893

Hatfield, Henry Rand. **Modern Accounting:** Its Principles and Some of its Problems. 1916

Kehl, Donald. **Corporate Dividends:** Legal and Accounting Problems Pertaining to Corporate Distributions. 1941

Leake, P[ercy] D[ewe]. **Depreciation and Wasting Assets and Their Treatment in Assessing Annual Profit and Loss.** 1912

Lisle, George. **Accounting in Theory and Practice.** 1900

Matheson, Ewing. **The Depreciation of Factories, Mines and Industrial Undertakings and Their Valuation.** 1893

Montgomery, Robert H. **Auditing Theory and Practice.** 1912

Norton, George Pepler. **Textile Manufacturers' Book-Keeping for the Counting House, Mill and Warehouse.** 1894

Paton, William A[ndrew] and Russell A[lger] Stevenson. **Principles of Accounting.** 1916

Pixley, Francis W[illiam]. **Auditors:** Their Duties and Responsibilities Under the Joint-Stock Companies Acts and the Friendly Societies and Industrial and Provident Societies Acts. 1881

Reiter, Prosper, Jr. **Profits, Dividends and the Law.** 1926

Scott, DR. **Theory of Accounts.** 1925

Scovell, Clinton H. **Interest as a Cost.** 1924

Sells, Elijah Watt. **The Natural Business Year and Thirteen Other Themes.** 1924

Soulé, Geo[rge]. **Soulé's New Science and Practice of Accounts.** 1903

Sprouse, Robert T[homas]. **The Effect of the Concept of the Corporation on Accounting.** 1976

Zeff, Stephen A., editor. **Asset Appreciation, Business Income and Price-Level Accounting: 1918-1935.** 1976